ARIZONIANA

Stories From Old Arizona

by

Marshall Trimble

Arizona's Official State Historian

The Arizona Trilogy — Volume 3

GOLDEN WEST ☼ PUBLISHERS

Front cover art: *The Cavalry Cook with Water* by Frederic Remington

About the Illustrator

Jack Graham's black-and-white illustrations lend a distinctive note to this collection. Having an interest in art from his earliest recollection, Jack has long worked toward a career as an illustrator. His formal art training includes studies at Arizona State University and a Bachelor of Fine Arts degree in illustration from Utah State University. Jack now makes his home in Scottsdale, Arizona.

Oher books by Marshall Trimble:
Arizona Adventure
In Old Arizona
Marshall Trimble's Official Arizona Trivia

Many of these stories appeared earlier in one of the following publications: *Phoenix Metro Magazine, Arizona Highways, Arizona Republic's Arizona Magazine, Scottsdale Progress' Saturday Magazine*

Library of Congress Cataloging-in-Publication Data

Trimble, Marshall.
Arizoniana : Stories from old Arizona / as told by Marshall Trimble.
   p. cm.
Includes index.
 ISBN 1-885590-89-X (alk. paper)
1. Arizona—History—Anecdotes. 2. Arizona—Biography—Anecdotes. I. Title
F811.6.T75 2002
979.1—dc21

Printed in the United States of America

3rd Printing © 2004

Golden West Publishers
4113 N. Longview Ave.
Phoenix, AZ 85014, USA
(602) 265-4392

For complete Table of Contents and excerpts/sample recipes from all Golden West titles, visit our website: goldenwestpublishers.com

To
Roger

"I gotta be the luckiest dad in the world to have a kid like you."

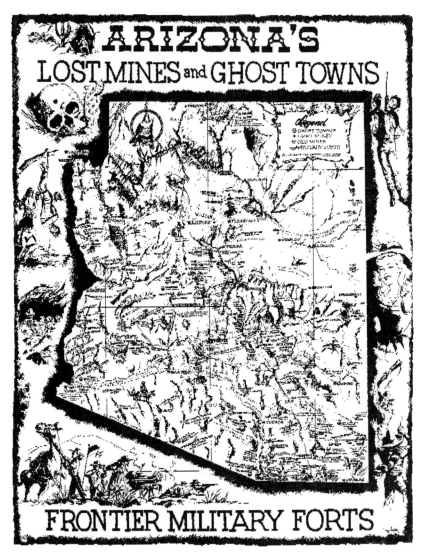

ARIZONA'S LOST MINES and GHOST TOWNS

FRONTIER MILITARY FORTS

Contents

Table of Contents (continued)

Meet the Author!

This Arizona native is one of the state's most popular and colorful personalities. He's the state's favorite native son and is often referred to as the "Will Rogers of Arizona."

Marshall Trimble is also one of the most sought-after banquet and convention speakers in the state. He's appeared on ABC's *Good Morning America,* The Nashville Network, and CBS's *This Morning.* The cowboy singer-story-teller has performed with Rex Allen, Waylon Jennings, Jerry Lee Lewis and the Oak Ridge Boys. He's also appeared in Las Vegas, Los Angeles and San Francisco.

(Photo by Simone Bibeau)

While enjoying the reputation of being one of America's most colorful raconteurs of this nation's colorful folk history, Marshall Trimble is also considered the dean of Arizona historians. He taught Arizona and Western history at the college level for 27 years, and is Arizona's Official State Historian.

Marshall Trimble

His books include the award-winning *Arizona: A Cavalcade of History; A Roadside History of Arizona,* and *Arizona: A Panoramic History of a Frontier State.* He was editor of the popular *Arizona Trivia* board game and scriptwriter for the award-winning *Portrait of America* series on Arizona. His stories and cowboy poems have appeared in such magazines as *Arizona Highways, Western Horseman* and *The American Cowboy.* His cassette recording, *Legends in Levis,* is a popular-selling collection of old cowboy songs. Other books published by Golden West Publishers include *In Old Arizona, Arizoniana* and *Arizona Trivia.*

Marshall Trimble began his career as a folk singer during the 1960s and today appears on stage, radio and television as a humorist and storyteller of Arizona and the West.

Marshall Trimble

Arizona's Official State Historian

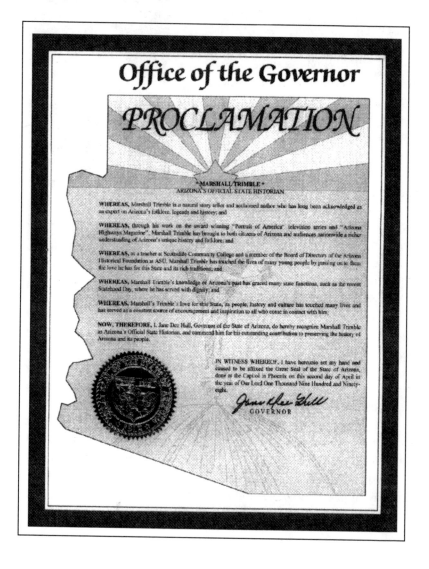

Savvy Sayin's and Sage Observations I Wish I'd Said

"I have a good memory, it's just short."

"A penny saved is a penny earned . . .
unless the IRS finds out about it."

"Hot weather makes people stick together."

"He's so tough he shaves with a Monkey Ward lawn mower."

"He was so mean that when his mama gave him his first
rattles she left the snake attached."

"A slick way to out-figure a fellar is to get him to figuring you
figure he'll figure you aren't really figuring
what you want him to figure you figure."

"If we continue to slaughter our wildlife,
the forests will have to buy from the pet shops."

"I'm in favor of capital punishment.
If you're going to punish a guy, might as well
do something he won't forget."

"Prostitution is the only business I know where you get to
keep what you sell."

"If a man ain't nothin' else, then he's an artist. It's the only
thing he can claim to be that nobody else can claim he ain't."

"It's bad manners to correct an accomplished liar. Whenever I
tell a story, if it didn't happen, it could have . . .
Or should have."

"Can a girl who comes from Buffalo find happiness
with a boy who comes from normal parents?"

"It always rains after a dry spell."

"I know you believe you understand what you think I said,
but I'm not sure you realize that what you heard
is what I meant."

"His limitations are limitless."

"You'll get more with a kind word . . . and a gun,
than you will with just a kind word."

"Never give a heifer a bum steer."

"A pretty lady looks good wearing anything.
She can wear nothing and look even better."

"If I'd known I was going to live this long,
I'd a taken better care of myself."

"Arizona summers ain't *that* hot,
they're jest too damn long."

The "Country Music Has a Message" Department of Songs I Wish I'd Written:

"She Sang With Me; But Played With the Band"

"The Man From the Gas Company Turned My Woman On"

"You Don't Have To Be A Weight-lifter
to Have Dumbells for Kids"

"It Got Around to Me That She'd Been
Gettin' Around With Him"

"It's Your Fault the Kids Are Ugly"

"You Caught My Eye Last Night,
When Your Boyfriend Knocked It Out"

How They Dug the Gold

"I'm a hardrock miner an' I ain't afeard of ghosts
But my neck hair bristles like a prospector's quills
An' I knock my knuckles on the drift-set posts
When the Tommyknockers hammer on the caps an' sills
An' raise hallelujah with my pick and drills."

Back in 1850, when the New Mexico territory was created, the wild, untamed western portion that would become Arizona was sparsely populated by non-Indians. The only white community was Tucson. Word quickly trickled back east about the vast mineral riches. "If ya stumble on a rock, don't cuss it—cash it" or, "If ya wash yer face in the Hassa-yampa River ya can pan four ounces of gold dust from yer whiskers." Rumors—but each one sent thousands of would-be millionaires scurrying up hundreds of arroyos searching for the elusive *madre del oro.*

Placer gold, the kind you could mine with the toe of your boot, or a jackknife, soon played out and the day of the romantic jackass prospector evolved into the era of the hardrock miner.

In the early days of underground mining, highly skilled Cornish miners were imported to do the work. They called the close-knit miners, Cousin Jacks.

Before caged elevators came into use, miners were low-ered hundreds of feet into the murky depths in a big steel bucket—powered by a "burro engine," which lowered the bucket on a long cable. Since it was pitch dark, the men carried candles, at first. Later they wore tiny oil lamps on their caps. Two men worked as a team. One swung a nine-pound hammer, the other turned the drill. At the end of the shift they filled the holes with explosives and blasted out the rich ore.

It was dangerous work. Cave-ins trapped them causing a slow death with falling rocks crushing them to death in an instant. A broken cable could send helpless miners tumbling hundreds of feet to their death. Fires were common and feared the most. Death was a constant companion to these hard-rock miners.

Men who work where danger is a way of life have a tendency to embrace superstitions and habits that may seem odd or strange to an outsider. The miners believed, for example, that it was bad luck for a woman to go into a mine; that if a man's work clothes slipped off their hook in the change room he was going to fall into a hole; and if one's lamp didn't burn bright, it meant his wife was stepping out with another man.

Miners often put their trust in critters such as canaries, mules and rats. Poisonous gasses drifting through the tun-nels were a silent killer. Since canaries couldn't live long in the foul air, miners took them down into the hole. When the canary died it was time to get out, pronto. Mules could be prophetic. One time a mule headed out of the tunnel before the ore car was filled. While the miner went out to retrieve the animal the whole place caved in. Rats also had a keen sense of danger. Like leaving a sinking ship, "When the rats move out, so does the miner."

The most unusual of the Cornish miner's superstitions were the Tommyknockers. These mischievous little people stood only two feet tall, had big heads, long arms, wrinkled faces and white beards.

It was said the little sprites sneaked into the luggage of the Cornishmen as they left for America. Once here, they infiltrated the mines by hiding in the miners lunch boxes. Old timers said the Tommyknockers communicated with miners by tapping on the walls with a code similar to the one devised by Samuel Morse. Sometimes these tappings warned of pending disaster while others gave direction to rich pockets of ore. Many a hard-rock miner swore his life was saved only because he'd heeded the tappings of the little people and made a hasty exit. Tommyknockers were credited with locating many a bonanza. But you had to listen to the Tommy-knocks. Miners claimed if one heard a "tap, tap," it meant "that's it" or "dig here;" whereas, "tap, tap, tap" meant "don't dig there."

Then, there was old Gassy Thompson. He was assisted in his quest for gold, not only by the Tommyknockers but by a diamondback rattlesnake and a pet dog appropriately named Digby. One day he killed a big "she-male rattler" and noticed a baby crawling away. He took the little critter home and made a pet of it. The snake came to love Gassy and followed him everywhere. Gassy believed that since the snake was much closer to the ground it could spot the gold he missed (Makes sense to me!). So he trained the little feller to recognize gold. Whenever the snake found a nugget it would coil up and start rattling. Gassy claimed on one occasion the snake found a $2,700 pocket of gold.

During hot weather Gassy would search for gold in the cool confines of abandoned gold mines. He learned to communicate with the Tommyknockers and they would tell him where to look for the gold. Then he'd bring in Digby to do the manual labor.

Skeptics were prone to doubt Gassy Thompson's methods of finding gold but one thing is certain—he always found more rich pockets of gold than all the other desert rats put together.

Don't Go Fer Yer Six-Shooter Unless Yer Shore It's There!

Bill Downing was one of the most disliked fellows in old Arizona. He was moody, morose, bad-tempered, sullen and surly. That was when he was sober. He got downright mean and ugly when he was drinking ol' red-eye.

He was so unpopular that even members of his gang couldn't stand him. It's a historical fact that one time when Bill and several other members of the Alvord gang were languishing in the Tombstone jail on a train robbery charge, a crony broke in and freed the other outlaws but left Bill locked in his cell.

He was so bad that the only thing good one could say about him was he wasn't as despicable sometimes as he was usually.

If I seem to have painted ol' Bill with a jaundiced brush, it's because he likely would have wanted it that way. If he had any good qualities history has mislaid them like some old lost gold mine.

It's been rumored Bill rode with the Sam Bass gang in his younger days. Somewhere along the way he married a young lady from a good family in Texas. She withered and died while he was in the Territorial Prison at Yuma serving time for robbing a train.

After Bill got out of prison in 1907 he returned to Willcox, one of his earlier haunts, and opened up a saloon called The Free and Easy. It soon became the hangout for all the nefarious scalawags in that part of Cochise County. Arizona law had banned women from "loitering" in saloons but that didn't bother Bill. He employed an assortment of shady ladies to drink with the customers. The girls were highly skilled pickpockets, too. Victims were reluctant to complain because of Bill's reputation as a gunslinger. He boldly threatened the life of anyone who might cause him a return visit to the Yuma prison. The law was laying for a chance to arrest Bill but he had terrorized the folks in Willcox to such a degree that none would file charges. Bill's downfall began the night he beat up one of the girls. When she complained to the local constable, Bud Snow, a warrant was issued.

Now the best time to serve a warrant on a miscreant like Bill Downing is early morn' before he's had a chance to indulge more of the "hair of the dog that bit him."

The constable enlisted Arizona Ranger, Billy Speed, in arresting Bill. On the morning of August 5, 1908 the two lawmen stood in front of The Free and Easy Saloon and called on Bill to step outside. The old outlaw ignored the first request, continuing to drink with a few other early morning imbibers. After the second demand Downing turned and headed for the back door. About that same time the Arizona Ranger, Billy Speed, armed with a 30-40 Winchester, headed around the side of the building. The two turned a corner at the same moment and faced each other in the classic Old West confrontation.

Bill Downing, a left-hander, reached for his left holster where his six-shooter was supposed to be stashed. At the same time the Ranger raised his Winchester and fired. Bill never got off a shot. The surprised desperado had reached in his pocket and came up empty. It seems that when he turned to leave the bar one of the patrons had picked Bill's pocket. The notorious outlaw, who swore he'd never be taken, died empty-handed on the streets of Willcox. A coroner's verdict ruled the killing justified while locals cheered Bill's demise. Even in death nobody cared to say something nice about Bill Downing.

The incident was the inspiration for an axiom that still holds true in old Arizona—don't go fer yer six-shooter unless yer shore its there!

Will Rogers in Arizona –
"If That Was MY Lake . . ."

One of the many things that strikes newcomers as peculiar about Arizona is our insistence on referring to dry stream beds as rivers.

Just the other day a tourist said to me, "Sir, your creeks have more running water than your rivers."

Well, he had me there, but I went on to point out the advantages of catching "native desert trout" in the Rio Seco. "They're already fried and ready to eat when you catch 'em," I explained. "The only trouble is that when you try to hook 'em, they've been known to kick dust in your face." His curiosity suitably aroused, I solemnly continued, "An old timer up at Globe told me about a flash flood that drowned a whole species of native trout."

The damming of Arizona's great rivers has made them a mere shadow of their old turbulent days. But still those irreverent rivers are plenty capable of kicking off their hobbles and running wild as a spring colt.

Personally, my favorite river is the Gila. Its Spanish name translates roughly as "a steady going to or coming from someplace." And that's what the old river did for several thousand years, though today it is one of our driest rivers. Before it was dammed, it meandered across Arizona, sustaining a rich lifestyle for the Pima Indians, and before that the prehistoric Hohokam. In time, Spanish missionaries and soldiers camped on its banks and Mexican vaqueros gathered wild cattle on its brushy floodplain.

During the California gold rush would-be millionaires on their way to the promised land used to float down the Gila, saving themselves the hazards crossing the fearsome desert sands.

It's been said that in 1849, a Mrs. Howard gave birth to a baby boy while floating down the Gila on a raft. He was named Gila, in honor of his birthplace, and the folklore has it that he was the first Anglo baby born within the boundaries of what would become Arizona.

Three years earlier, Lieutenant George Stoneman of the Mormon Battalion experimented with transporting military goods on the Gila. The raft, with Stoneman on board, was launched amidst as much ceremony as one could manage in the wilds of Arizona. A short distance downstream the raft began to sink and Lieutenant Stoneman, a brave sea captain to the very end, went down with his ship. then walked ashore. As far as we know that was the last time there was any government sponsored navigation on the Gila.

Wet years and dry came in their usual cycles just as they have for thousands of years and the venerable Gila continued to go its own way in its own time.

In 1885, the Thirteenth Territorial Legislature appropriated $12,000 to build a bridge across the Gila. The citizens of Florence were tired of the river's fickle behavior.

No sooner had the bridge been built and dedicated when the irrepressible Gila changed its course, swung out into the desert and left that bridge standing all alone.

In 1930, the Bureau of Reclamation completed the construction of Coolidge Dam on the upper Gila. The bureau had researched the river thoroughly before deciding where the dam should be built. Unfortunately, however, the years reviewed in the study were unusually wet and a series of years after the dam was finished were unusually dry. Well, the Gila got stubborn and refused to form the reservoir that was supposed to take shape behind the dam. It took 50 years, in fact, for San Carlos Lake to fill.

Will Rogers, at the dedication ceremony attended by President Coolidge in 1930, looked at the grassy lake bed and said, "If that was *my* lake, I'd mow it!"

The Great Boundary Fiasco

One of the major problems arising from the War with Mexico (1846-48) was that neither side knew exactly which territory had been won and lost. Only a few hard-scrabble mud adobe villages existed in the rugged, unexplored regions of today's Southwest. It was a blank on the map of North America. The Mexican government had only a vague idea of the sparsely populated land, as no accurate map was in existence. The only known chart of the area was drawn by James Disturnall in 1847, and it proved to be inaccurate.

Article V of the Treaty of Guadalupe Hidalgo stipulated that a joint Mexican-American boundary survey would establish an international border-line between the two nations. The Mexicans, to their credit, selected one of their top engineers, General Pedro Garcia Conde, to represent their interests while the U.S. chose as their representative John Russell Bartlett, of Rhode Island, a part-owner of a bookstore.

Bartlett, scion from old and respected New England stock and a staunch member of the Whig party, was appointed when Zachery Taylor and the Whigs came into power in 1849. He had requested an appointment as ambassador to Denmark, but when that position was filled by another, he graciously accepted the Boundary Commissioner's job as his party's second choice. The first was John C. Fremont, the Great Pathfinder, but when he resigned to become U.S. Senator from the new state of California, Bartlett was appointed.

Actually, Bartlett was the fifth man selected. Former President James Polk had asked army major William Emory to take the job but the officer declined because he didn't wish to resign his commission. That was unfortunate because the 38-year-old soldier was probably the most brilliant topographical engineer in the U.S. He did agree, however, to be chief astronomer and cartographer on the expedition.

Polk's next appointee, Ambrose Servier, died before the Senate could confirm him and John B. Weller became choice number three. Weller, a capable man, had just been defeated in a political race and was in need of employment. Since the appointment was political, Weller was quickly replaced when President Taylor took office.

Bartlett was not unhappy at being appointed Boundary Commissioner. By his own words he had led a sedentary life and wanted to travel for a change. He also had a great interest in American Indians, whom he'd never seen in their native habitat. He saw this as an excellent opportunity to write a book on the subject. For the next two and one-half years, he and his expensive entourage would travel extensively in the Southwest, Mexico and California spending as little time as possible on the business of establishing a boundary line on the 1,500-mile U.S.-Mexican border. But, he did write one heck of a book on the area.

When the War ended in 1848, the U.S. acquired about half of the Mexican Republic. This vast new acquisition, including Texas, (which won its independence from Mexico in 1836 and joined the Union in 1845) increased the size of the U.S. by one-third. The treaty line, as yet unsurveyed, was to begin three marine leagues out in the Gulf of Mexico, then up the deepest channel of the Rio Grande to the southern boundary of the territory of New Mexico; thence west for three degrees of longitude (some 178 miles), proceed north to the nearest branch of the Gila River and down the deepest channel to the junction of the Colorado River; from there the line was to run across to a point one marine league (3.5 miles) south of the Bay of San Diego.

Senator John H. Clarke, of Bartlett's home state of Rhode Island, secured his appointment as Boundary Commissioner. Clark's son was immediately put on the commission's payroll. Bartlett was besieged by a band of eager adventurous young fire-eating heroes who wanted to go West. The gold rush to California was at its height, something that inspired many would-be millionaires to want to go along for the ride. Most of these seem to have been endorsed by influential politicians and Bartlett was too much an amateur at handling such things to say no. He was forced to choose some 100 inexperienced white-collar, government boondogglers. Surveyor Andrew B. Gray later said four-fifths were utterly useless. Bartlett appointed his brother George, Commissary. An unwise choice, for George immediately set about purchasing some $100,000 in useless pieces of equipment at inflated prices. Too late, it was discovered George had purchased barrels of flour, infested with weevils and pork, crawling with worms. He seems to have amassed a small fortune in kickbacks from unscrupulous government contractors. Fortunately for the hapless Boundary Commissioner, he was saddled with a capable surveyor, Gray, who was ably assisted by Major Emory and Lieutenant Amiel W. Whipple of the Army Corps Topographical Engineers.

After a lengthy delay, the Rhode Island scholar and his entourage of 111 civilians and 85 military personnel arrived at the dusty town of El Paso del Norte (Juarez), population, some 3,000, in November, 1850.

The scholarly New Englander had not been in El Paso del Norte long when he got his first taste of raw frontier justice. Edward Clarke, son of the Rhode Island senator, was knifed to death at a fandango by a band of border ruffians. Eight or nine desperadoes were arrested and brought to trial before a judge and jury, of the roughest looking, heavily-armed Mexicans and Americans he'd yet seen.

The courtroom was jammed with a boisterous crowd of curious spectators attired with wide-brimmed sombreros, wearing serapes or overcoats and smoking corn husk cigarillos. They, too, were heavily armed with Bowie knives, pistols and rifles. Three of the accused, all former members of Bartlett's commission, were found guilty and hanged that same day. The leader of the gang was caught later and hanged from the same tree. The other rascals got the message and made a hasty exit from the region.

At El Paso, Bartlett made the acquaintance of the distinguished Mexican Boundary Commissioner, General Pedro Garcia Conde. It didn't take long for the smooth-talking general to use his superior knowledge in engineering to full advantage over his American counterpart.

One of the purposes of the treaty was to allow room for the building of a road to California following the road surveyed by the Mormon Battalion during the war. The line was to run from a point eight miles north of El Paso del Norte. The only map available was James Disturnall's and it had located El Paso on the wrong latitude, placing the town some 42 miles further north, and the Rio Grande 100 miles further east than it actually was. The persuasive Mexican general convinced Bartlett the line as shown on the map should be used, regardless of errors. All the American engineers protested loudly, claiming that the line should run eight miles north of El Paso del Norte, regardless of what the map said. Besides, they argued, the map was used only to show that the line should run eight miles north of town and nothing more.

Southerners were especially indignant over Bartlett's surrendering some 6,000 square miles of land, much of it in the fertile Mesilla Valley, to Mexico.

Bartlett and Conde reached a compromise whereby the Mexicans would give up some longitude for the extra latitude. The Americans would get the rich Santa Rita del Cobre Mines some 90 miles to the northwest and the Mexicans would get the rich, fertile Mesilla Valley. Bartlett may have been further swayed when Mexican citizens of the old town of Mesilla prevailed upon him to keep their community in Mexico. The American engineers, mostly Southerners, saw Bartlett's act as another case of Northerners disregarding the rights of Southerners, in this case a southern road to California. The new compromise did not provide room to build a southern railroad (this would later necessitate another land acquisition, the Gadsden Purchase).

In order to finalize the agreement, both the commissioners and the surveyors had to sign. But surveyor Andrew Gray was absent so Bartlett appointed Lieutenant Amiel Whipple surveyor ad interim, then ordered him to sign the agreement. This done, the party moved on to other business.

Andrew Gray, of Texas, surveyor for the Boundary Commission, was eminently well-qualified for the job and he was interested in a southern railroad line. Gray, along with Emory and Whipple of the Army Corps of Topographical Engineers, who were assisting him, agreed that the land being given the Mexicans was vital to the building of a railroad to California.

Gray refused to sign the agreement and both he and Bartlett wrote letters to officials in Washington to defend their positions. Since it took months for letters to get from one point to the other, the matter went unresolved and the parties decided to continue the survey.

Bartlett's primary mission as Boundary Commissioner seems to have been directed more towards an ethnological study of the natives of the region. Boundary matters took a back seat. He horse-collared every stray Indian encountered along the trail and subjected the puzzled fellow to a series of lengthy tests on the correct pronunciation of the native tongue, which he wrote down in phonetic English.

His first encounter was with a friendly, rather heavy, Lipan Apache chief who bore a strong resemblance to the erstwhile presidential candidate, Lewis Cass. The chief seems to have dealt a shattering blow to Bartlett's romantic image of the "noble red savage," when he stubbornly demanded whiskey and was nonplused when told none was available. Bartlett assured the chief that he carried no ardent spirits but only drank water. The chief finally accepted, with reservations, a cup of coffee as a consolation for his cooperation.

This would not be the only time Bartlett was to learn something about the realities of business intercourse in the Southwest. At the Pima villages along the Gila, one chief insisted on sampling the various bottles until he choked and sputtered on a bottle of diarrhea medicine. During a parley, Mangas Coloradas, the great Apache chief, demanded a glass of whiskey. Again, Bartlett insisted, truthfully, that none was available. In his quest for the customary diplomatic toddy, Mangas, too, insisted on sampling all the ingredients contained in bottles, including vinegar and catsup.

In a noble attempt to soothe the chief's ruffled feathers, and amid much pomp and ceremony, Bartlett presented Mangas with a frock coat, lined with scarlet, decorated with ornate buttons. Included, at the chief's request, were a pair of Mexican pantaloons, slit from the knee down and lined with a row of elaborate buttons and lined on the outside with a strip of red cloth. This piece of resplendent high fashion was topped off with a white shirt and a bright scarlet sash made of silk. Bartlett's New England ire was raised when the chief insisted on leaving the shirttail hanging out.

Dining with the Apaches was another event that put the generous Boundary Commissioner's patience to the test. The selected guests, all chiefs, would feast with great gusto, then refill their plates and pass them back to friends and relatives who were hovering about the dining area.

Bartlett continued to maintain a conciliatory attitude towards all Indians he encountered and literally wore them down with his incessant language recording sessions. For those who cooperated, he presented with much fanfare, a prize of sorts. Also, a letter was presented testifying to the friendliness or trustworthiness of the carrier. The letters were addressed: "To Whom it May Concern," and were decorated with a red ribbon and impressive seal. The Indians were well-pleased with such documents and displayed them proudly. At times, some particular roguish fellow would insist on having one, so the Americans handled the delicate situation in grand style by presenting the same elaborate document but writing instead, "He's a damn big rascal, don't trust him out of your sight." No doubt this served to educate some other unsuspecting American party as to the true nature of the bearer.

Bartlett's "temperance movement" offended the natives, who were used to such amenities in the normal course of socializing and cooperating with the Americans. Soon they took to running off the livestock as a means of demonstrating their displeasure. This caused many delays and created an interesting turnabout as the Americans, rather than their Mexican counterparts, were continually doing things *mañana*. No doubt, General Conde and his colleagues were quite amused to see the Americans procrastinating because their leader was off interrogating Indians for his language collection or trying to purchase replacement stock.

Bartlett clashed with Mexicans and Indians on another point, one in which he had little understanding. The two cultures had been at war for several generations and the taking of captives for slavery purposes was a reality of life on the frontier. When Mangas brought two captives into the American camp, Bartlett confiscated the pair and refused to pay for them. The chief was quite vexed that this naive Yankee not only refused him a drink but now purloined his personal property. He was appeased somewhat when the Americans slipped some expensive trade goods to a Mexican teamster who, in turn, handed them over to the Apache chieftain.

When the Boundary Commissioner spotted a beautiful, young Mexican girl being held captive by a band of Mexican traders, his puritanical morality was outraged. The girl, Inez Gonzales, revealed that she had been stolen from her family in Mexico by Apaches and then sold to the traders. He impounded the girl and appointed himself as her guardian angel until she could be returned safely to her family. As further proof of his devotion to youthful virtue, he gallantly renamed a nearby watering hole, Inez's Spring. Then he decided to deliver Inez personally, on a very gentle mule, to the town of Santa Cruz, where a joyful reunion with family and friends was held. The entire community applauded the chivalrous Boundary Commissioner with great elan. However, Bartlett's self-esteem suffered a setback the next morning when he discovered his supplies pilfered by the locals.

Bartlett literally abandoned his beleaguered surveyors

for 44 days of severe hardships while making the grand gesture of returning young Inez to her parents. He then decided to go further south on a supply purchasing journey that took him clear to Acapulco. From there he traveled north as far as San Francisco happily scribbling notes and gathering much information for his journals, but no supplies.

Finally, the itinerate Boundary Commissioner returned to San Diego where he rejoined Lieutenant Whipple and his men. From there the party traveled inland towards Arizona. Upon reaching the old presidio at Tubac, Bartlett's faith in mankind was further shattered when he discovered that the fair maiden, Inez Gonzales, was living in sin with a Mexican officer. The Boundary Commissioner was convinced that the poor waif was once again a victim of involuntary servitude. The officer was somewhat confounded, but polite, at this sanctimonious invasion of his household. Inez, too, was a bit puzzled at the Boundary Commissioner's offer to return her once more to her parents' home. The reunion ended when the two promised Bartlett they would join him later on the trail and that Inez would rejoin her parents. Not surprisingly, they failed to keep the appointment.

By this time Bartlett's incompetence and mismanagement had caught up with him. Critics charged him with using government transportation for private use, mismanagement of public funds and general negligence. Some $500,000 was spent on the survey of which only $100,000 was spent on the actual work. His critics in Washington were able to table any further spending and Bartlett's Boundary Commission died a natural death. The issue over the disputed Mesilla Valley was not resolved and the U.S. and Mexico were on the brink of another war for a brief period. The matter was finally resolved when James Gadsden reached an agreement with Mexico in 1853, whereby the land in dispute and Arizona south of the Gila River became a part of the United States, thus marking this nation's last continental acquisition.

John Russell Bartlett went home to New England and composed a two-volume work on his travels. During those turbulent days when his commission was in political hot water, one of his detractors characterized Bartlett's writings as the most expensive guidebook ever published. And, so it might have been, but his narrative has withstood the test of time and is recognized today as a classic piece of primary research on the pristine Southwest.

Con Men of Yesteryear

Today's disreputable land promoters selling lakeshore lots on edges of mirages are mere amateurs when compared to the wheeler dealers of yesteryear.

The lawless Arizona territory attracted the wide gamut of frontier con men ranging from tin horn gamblers to stock swindlers.

One was Doctor Richard Flower. Doc Flower wasn't really a doctor. He earned his living for a time selling cure-all bottled medicine. Although Doc Flower claimed his recipe could cure everything from baldness to toothaches, it really had no redeeming medicinal value. It did contain enough alcohol to mellow its imbibers enough that nobody felt ripped off. Anyhow, that's how he came to be called Doctor Flower.

Doc Flower eventually grew weary of small-time scheming and decided to play for higher stakes. Fortunes were being made in the Arizona mines and since Doc Flower didn't have a bonafide mine of his own, he decided to create one.

He'd never been to Arizona and wouldn't have known a nugget from rolled oats but that didn't stop him. He erected a phony, movie-set looking mine complete with headframe east of Globe, bought a few samples of ore from a producing mine and headed back east to promote his strike.

He called the company the Spendazuma, something that indicates ol' Doc Flower did at least have a wry sense of humor. Mazuma was a slang for money; so in effect he was promoting the "Spend-yer-money" mine and nobody caught on. Would-be millionaires were waiting in line to buy stock in Doc's mine.

The balloon burst when a reporter from the *Arizona Republican* (today's *Republic*), named George Smalley, rode out to have a look at this mine. The property was being guarded by one of Doc's hirelings, a hard-bitten character named Alkali Tom. Tom tried his best to keep the snoopy reporter from getting too close to Doc's imaginary gold mine but Smalley was not to be denied. Workers were about as scarce as horse flies in December and Smalley became suspicious. A closer examination revealed the whole setup was a phony.

When Smalley's exposé made the papers, Doc's lawyer indignantly threatened to sue for $100,000 and demanded a retraction. Smalley could hardly keep from laughing, so they offered him $5,000 to rewrite the story and admit he made a mistake. When the spunky reporter assumed a pugilist's pose, the lawyer retreated and Doc Flower's blossoming Spendazuma scheme withered away.

Bret Harte spent enough time around mining camps to become an authority on the art of selling worthless claims to unsuspecting tenderfeet. He wrote rather poetically on the subject:

> *"The ways of a man with a maid may be strange yet simple and tame when compared to a man with a mine when buying or selling the same."*

One over-zealous promoter distributed brochures back

east extolling the mineral riches in the Bradshaw Mountains. On the cover was a picture of an ocean-going, ore-laden vessel steaming down the mighty Hassayampa River.

Unscrupulous prospectors upgraded their dubious mining properties in a manner contrary to nature by a process known as salting. Since gold was malleable, it could be loaded in a shotgun shell and impregnated into the rocky walls of a worthless tunnel creating a glittering Golconda.

One careless victim bought a silver mine laden with chunks of blackened native silver from an honest-looking dealer. A closer examination of one of the nuggets revealed the partially melted words: United States of America.

Sometimes the property owner became the victim in cases of salting. One of the most unusual happened to a man named Julian, who owned a rather large operation.

When a rich body of ore was found in one of the tunnels, the price of the stock rose dramatically on the local exchange. Three employees offered to sell their inflated stock back to the boss. That alone should have made Julian wary but he eagerly purchased the stock. A few days later the "vein" played out and the stock went back down. Julian lost a tidy sum on the stock drop and became suspicious. When the three Irish miners were asked if they had salted the mine, each innocently denied guilt.

"Would you swear to that on the Holy Bible?" Julian asked. The miners shrugged their shoulders and agreed, whereupon Julian produced an ornate Bible and had each man declare himself innocent. "I believe those men," Julian declared. "No good Irish-Catholic would dare place his hand upon the Holy Bible and deliberately lie."

Julian might have gone right on believing their innocence had he not dropped the Bible while returning it to the bookshelf. The book jacket flopped open to the title page. Julian looked once, blinked then looked again. Instead of Holy Bible, it said, Webster's Dictionary. Those Irish miners had anticipated what Julian would do and had "salted" his Holy Bible.

Capitol Chaos

During times like these it pays to remember, there have always been times like these. Ex-governor Evan Mecham is but one more in a long line of chief executives who have raised the ire of political opponents; been subjected to loud public outcries; battled the legislature; tangled with members of their own party; and been the victim of a hostile press.

It all began back in 1863 when Arizona became a territory. President Abraham Lincoln appointed John Gurley of Ohio as the territory's first governor and, soon after learning of the appointment, Gurley up and died.

The next appointee, John Goodwin, stayed around just long enough to take exception to the rough-hewn citizenry and a capitol building of un-chinked logs and dirt floor. He opted to run for territorial delegate and returned to the comfortable environs of Washington, D.C.

The third governor was Richard McCormick. He stood only 5' 5" and was known as Tricky Dick to his political adversaries. McCormick incurred the wrath of the Prescott press when he maneuvered to move the capital from the mile-high city to Tucson. "His Littleness," wrote editor John Marion of the *Prescott Miner*, "who by soft soap and flunkyism, has wormed his way into the gubernatorial chair of a territory he has helped to impoverish." Despite the cries of fraud and bribery by angry Prescottonians, the capital was relocated to a small adobe building in the Old Pueblo.

John C. Fremont, the renowned Pathfinder, was another governor who felt the rancor of the Arizona citizenry and press. He was appointed governor to pay off an old political debt. Fremont, however, wasn't all that thrilled with the job and spent most of his time back East promoting various mining schemes. In 1882, succumbing to public pressure, Fremont was removed from office.

Conrad Zulick, the first Democrat to hold office, began his tenure under the most unusual circumstances, to say the least. Zulick, a lawyer, was locked up in the Mexican town of Nacozari when appointed. Doc Donovan, a rather colorful character from Cochise County, was sent across the border to make the rescue. The heroic scene read like the script of a 1940s B Western: Doc rode into Nacozari in the middle of the night and crept stealthily up to the place where Zulick was being held. As luck would have it, the guards were all fast asleep. Zulick was smuggled out the back door to a waiting wagon and driven to the border. The next day, Doc drove the new Arizona governor into Tombstone where he was greeted by a cheering throng of well-wishers.

Lewis Wolfley, a diminutive man with an abrasive personality, battled Democrats, fellow-Republicans, the press and the public. After 16 stormy months in office, he was forced, by his own party, to resign. For what it's worth,

Wolfley was the only bachelor to be appointed governor.

Statehood, in 1912, didn't change things much. Extreme dislike for the power held by territorial governors inspired fathers of the Arizona constitution to severely limit the powers of the governor. A vast majority of Arizonans were registered Democrats in those days so a victory in the Democratic primary was tantamount to winning the office. Democrats controlled the legislature and the governor's office most of the time but that was no guarantee of harmony. Having nothing to fear from the weak Republicans, minority Democrats divided into factions, battling the governor at every turn. Governors were about as welcome in the legislature as a sheepman at a cattleman's convention.

Regardless, there was never a shortage of aspirants for the office of governor. As a result of a hotly contested race in the election of 1916, Arizonans got two governors for the price of one. Democrat incumbent George W.P. Hunt and Republican challenger Tom Campbell both claimed victory after the latter out-polled the former by 30 votes.

Although Campbell, a Republican, was inaugurated on January 1, 1917, Hunt demanded a recount. He stubbornly refused to vacate the governor's office and held his own swearing-in ceremony. While Hunt occupied the governor's office, Campbell ran the state out of the kitchen in his home. The state treasurer and auditor, both Democrats, announced they wouldn't honor checks and claims approved by Campbell. When the state legislature convened both men came to the podium to deliver the state of the state address.

A few weeks later Superior Court Judge Rawghlie Stanford ruled Campbell the winner. Hunt appealed to the State Supreme Court and in December, 1917, was declared the winner. It seems many Democrats marked an "X" choosing to vote a straight ticket, but cast their vote for Campbell. Clearly, they wished to vote for all the Democrats except Hunt, but the court voided those ballots and that was enough to throw the election to Hunt.

Campbell, who had served for 11 months, was forced to return his pay and vacate the governor's office. He was later elected to two terms. Between the years 1911 to 1934 Hunt, a consummate politician, won the governor's race seven times in ten tries, something that inspired humorist Will Rogers to dub him Arizona's "perennial governor."

How the Nermernuh Finally Got Respect

Long before the white people migrated to the vast lands —across the wide Missouri—and added a new dimension to the struggle for supremacy, native tribes battled continuously for the most desirable lands.

As a rule, three things could happen to a weaker tribe and all were bad. At worst they were exterminated. If they escaped that, assimilation might occur or, as was often the case, they were driven to some less desirable area such as the arid, inhospitable deserts of the Great Basin and the Southwest. Many times, tribes were able to adapt to the harsh lands, turning a disadvantageous situation into a positive one, and gaining their greatest glory as warriors. The Apaches are a classic example. Driven into the barren deserts and brawny mountains of Arizona, New Mexico and the Mexican Republic by more powerful Plains tribes during the 1300s, they became masters in guerrilla warfare.

Perhaps even more dramatic was a tribe of people from the Shoshonian language group called the *Nermernuh,* a name which meant, in their language, The People. The Nermernuh were a humble, squatty, dark-skinned, common-looking tribe living in the northern Rockies. They were brow-beaten, pushed and shoved from region to region by stronger tribes. Eventually, they wound up on the high, desolate plains of West Texas, in a land called the *Llano Estacado,* or Staked Plains.

Then fate intervened.

In 1680, the Pueblo Indians living along the Rio Grande in New Mexico revolted and drove their Spanish conquerors out. During the retreat down the Rio Grande to El Paso del

Norte, horses got loose and wandered east into the Llano Estacado where they became the seed crop for some of the great herds of mustangs.

The arrival of the horse changed the lives of the Nermernuh overnight. The horse was not just a critter to be ridden, it became an object of worship. They quickly learned selective breeding, keeping only the best studs and gelding the rest. Now they could hunt mighty buffalo and challenge other tribes for supremacy. Children learned to ride almost before they learned to walk. They became the most feared raiders of their time, extending their former range by thousands of miles. Nermernuh raiding parties penetrated as far into Mexico as the Yucatan Peninsula. They became the scourge of the Pueblo and Hispanic peoples along the Rio Grande and the settlers in east Texas and along the Gulf Coast. Their success in battle seemed to make the Nermernuh more barbaric. They reveled in taking vengeance for hundreds of years of oppression. They were the first Plains Indians to acquire the horse and none ever adapted their culture to that animal so completely.

During the 1830s, American anthropologists observed these people and determined that the equine had been an integral part of the culture for thousands of years. In reality, the animal had been on the Plains only a little over a century.

For nearly 200 years the Nermernuh, recognized by other horse-Indians as *the* horse-Indians, were feared and respected.

In 1874, the U.S. Cavalry, after a long and hard-fought campaign, defeated the Nermernuh and located them on a reservation.

By now, you're probably wondering why the exploits of these remarkable people rings a note of familiarity but the name doesn't. That's because many of our Native American tribes are better known by the names given them by others, some of which weren't all that complimentary. The Nermernuh are better-known by a name given them by the Utes. Translated to English it means, "Man Who Goes Around Trying To Kill Me All The Time." In the language of the Utes, the word became synonymous with fear and terror in the Southwest for nearly two centuries. They were called Comanches.

Lieutenant Amiel Whipple's Good Deed

On a hot afternoon in 1849 not far from the Yuma River Crossing, a small party of Army Topographical Engineers came upon a young Indian girl wandering in the desert. She was nearly dead from exposure, hunger and thirst. Many would have left the youngster to her fate. It was a tough, unforgiving land where the strong survived and the weak perished.

The officer in charge was a kind, thoughtful man from Massachusetts, named Amiel Weeks Whipple. He'd only been in the Southwest a short time but had already developed a deep respect for the customs and culture of the native residents.

Whipple shared his canteen with the youngster, then gave her some food. Before she departed he presented her with a small mirror—a simple token of friendship and also something any young lady would surely cherish. She smiled and left to return to her people. Lieutenant Whipple went back to his job—that of surveying a boundary between Yuma and San Diego, marking the new land won in the recent war with Mexico.

Lieutenant Amiel Weeks Whipple, 31, was a member of the elite Army Corps of Topographical Engineers. He was among the select group of men given the task of marking the new 1,500-mile border between the United States and Mexico. The treaty makers had made a number of snafus and it was up to the engineers to straighten things out before open hostilities broke out again.

By December 10, 1849, the engineers had completed their work and the incident with the young Indian girl was long forgotten.

Two years later Whipple returned to survey the Gila River across Arizona. At the time, the Gila marked the boundary between United States and the Mexican Republic. Traveling west along the Gila, Whipple and his men, 47 in all, surveyed some 350 miles downstream. By December 22, 1851, they were about 60 miles east of Fort Yuma. Supplies were running low so Whipple decided to pack up his gear and head for the fort. He planned to spend Christmas within the friendly confines of the post before going on to San Diego to re-outfit.

Whipple and his men arrived at the Yuma River Crossing to find the fort abandoned. He was greeted by some 1,500 warriors with fire in their eyes. It was the same old story dating back to Spanish times. Some of the emigrants passing through had been abusing the natives. The army withdrew and the Yuma warriors seized both ferry boats. This river was a quarter of a mile wide and reached a depth of 30 feet, so Whipple and his men couldn't cross without the aid of the Indians. On Christmas Eve an interpreter warned Whipple that an attack was planned on his small party. The young officer and his men hastily fortified themselves using wagons and baggage as breastworks. The site where the engineers prepared to make their stand is believed to be near where the Yuma Territorial Prison stands today.

They kept a watchful eye throughout the night waiting for an attack that failed to materialize.

The next morning a delegation of war chiefs approached and asked for a parley. Whipple told them he would pay them well, $2 per man and $1 for each horse and mule, for ferrying the group across the river.

The warriors responded by demanding to know how much gold Whipple was carrying. Apparently the Yumas had learned something about the value of the Yankee dollar.

The situation was growing tense when the daughter of one of the war chiefs walked over and whispered something in her father's ear. He looked at Whipple for a moment then called the other warriors aside for a private parley. During the confab each cast a curious glance in Whipple's direction. Finally, the chief asked through an interpreter if Whipple had been at the Yuma Crossing two years earlier. Whipple replied in the affirmative and from the relief seen on the face of the interpreters he knew the crisis had passed. The mood shifted from open hostility to friendliness.

The Yumas not only ferried Whipple's party across the river but gave them escort all the way to San Diego's coastal mountains. It's a pretty good bet that Whipple's humanitarian act towards that little girl on the desert near Yuma two years earlier saved the lives of 47 men at the Yuma Crossing that Christmas Day in 1851.

The Case of
The Vanishing Train Robbers

On the evening of April 27, 1887, southern Arizona's only passenger train, the Sunset Express, was making its run toward Tucson. The train was a few minutes behind schedule, so the engineer gave her a little more steam to make up time. About 20 miles east of Tucson, the yellow streak from the headlight picked up a figure standing on the track waving a red lantern. About that same time, the big drive wheels ran over a torpedo. The bomb-like blast served as a warning of trouble on the line. He slammed on the brakes and stopped just before crashing into some upraised railroad ties jammed between the tracks.

Out of the darkness, rifle shots cracked and several holes suddenly appeared in the engine's boiler. Two masked men appeared beside the locomotive and ordered the engineer, Colonel Bill Harper, to step down off the train. They took him back to the express car and told him to have the Wells Fargo express messenger open the safe then unlock the door and get out.

"Or what?" The stubborn engineer asked.

"Or we blow it up," one of the bandits replied, holding up a stick of dynamite.

Inside the express car, messenger J.E. Smith heard the conversation and unlocked the safe. Then he removed $5,000, took it over to the cold, potbellied stove, lifted the lid and stuffed it in. The money safely hidden, the resourceful messenger unlocked the door and jumped out.

The robbers, members of the Doc Smart gang, found only a few scattered bills in the safe. Disappointed, they took their meager haul and after a few hurried instructions on how to run a locomotive from engineer Harper, climbed aboard and headed towards Tucson.

Later that night, in Tucson, when the Sunset Express failed to show, a relief train was sent out to search. About 15 miles east of Tucson, they discovered the abandoned steam engine and its ransacked express and mail cars. A few miles further on down the track, they found the anxious crew waiting by the passenger cars.

The next day a posse, led by Papago Indian trackers, went to where the engine was found to pick up the trail of Doc Smart and his desperados. They searched in vain but found no tracks. It was as if the gang had vanished into thin air.

Clever fellows, those outlaws, except they didn't get much loot since J. E. Smith had so cleverly hidden the money in the stove. The newspapers made a big deal out of it and Smith was a local celebrity for a spell.

On August 10, the Doc Smart gang struck again. Same train; same location; same operendus; and the same messenger, J. E. Smith.

This time the train didn't stop in time and the engine jumped the tracks and flipped over on its side on the edge of a steep embankment. Out of the darkness, the outlaws opened fire. One bullet passed under the nose of fireman R. T. Bradford, burning off part of his mustache. Engineer Jim Guthrie hopped out of the prostrate locomotive and tumbled over a steep bluff, landing in the top of a mesquite tree.

Doc and the boys weren't taking any chances this time. A stick of dynamite blew open the door of the express car. Inside was their old adversary, J. E. Smith. One of the robbers pointed the business end of his Colt .45 at the messenger and hissed, "Smitty, that stove racket don't go this time."

The gang got away with $3,000 that time and while lawmen scoured the Arizona country Doc Smart and the boys were livin' it up in Texas.

Things went so well the last time, two of the outlaws decided to rob the Southern Pacific outside El Paso, a couple of months later. Ironically, J. E. Smith was in the express car again. By now the feisty messenger was getting tired of getting heisted. This time he greeted the train robbers with his guns blazing. In a few brief but furious moments, outlaws Kid Smith (no relation) and Dick Meyers were laid out stone cold on the ground.

Smart detective work enabled lawmen in El Paso to locate the boarding house where the two outlaws were staying. Soon they rounded up the rest of the gang including the notorious Doc Smart.

Doc Smart was given a life sentence for his part in the three train robberies. Somehow he got his hands on a sixshooter and tried to commit suicide. Doc fired three slugs into his head but the soft lead collided with his hard head and couldn't penetrate. Doc Smart got nothing for his efforts except a severe headache.

It wasn't until several months later, after Doc Smart and his gang were captured at El Paso, that investigators learned what happened at the robbery east of Tucson. It was really quite simple. The outlaws merely rode the locomotive into the outskirts of town, then put the ol' iron-belly into reverse and sent it eastbound. The perforated boiler ran out of steam about ten miles down the track and that's where it was found—with no tell-tale tracks to follow.

Ol' Bill Williams

The picturesque town of Williams takes its name from Bill Williams Mountain that towers above and provides as beautiful high country setting for a community as can be found in America. It's a fitting place-name for ol' Bill Williams, the "greatest fur trapper of 'em all."

Ol' Bill was as colorful a man as any who ever forked a horse or mule and headed towards the setting sun. To those who knew the tireless old mountain man, he'd always seemed old and eccentric. His drunken sprees around Taos set the standard by which others tried to match but never could. Each season he rode alone into forbidding hostile

Indian country and returned safely, his pack mules laden with precious beaver pelts.

Ol' Bill was a tall, skinny, redhead, with a high-pitched voice, his body battle-scarred and worn. He was known to run all day with six traps on his back and never break into a sweat. He had a peculiar way of walking, it's been described as more closely resembling a stagger, and he never walked in a straight line. He fired his long-barreled, "Kicking Betsy" with unerring accuracy in what was described as a "double wobble." Ol' Bill never drew a steady bead with the heavy rifle. He let it drift back and forth across the target and squeezed the trigger at "jest" the right moment. On horseback, he wore his stirrups so short his knees bobbed just beneath his chin. He leaned forward in the saddle resembling a hunchback on horseback.

All these eccentricities enhanced his reputation as one of the Old West's most unforgettable characters. George Frederick Ruxton, an English adventurer who toured the West in the 1840s, wrote this colorful description of old Bill:

> "Williams always rode ahead, his body bent over his saddlehorn, across which rested a long, heavy rifle, his keen gray eyes peering from under the slouched brim of a flexible felt-hat, black and shining with grease. His buckskin hunting shirt, bedaubed until it had the appearance of polished leather, hung infolds over his bony carcass; his nether extremities being clothed in pantaloons of the same material . . . The old coon's face was sharp and thin, a long nose and chin hob-nobbing each other; and his head was always bent forward giving him the appearance of being hump-backed. He appeared to look neither to the right nor left, but, in fact, his little twinkling eye was everywhere. He looked at no one he was addressing, always seeming to be thinking of something else than the subject of his discourse, speaking in a whining, thin, cracked voice . . . His character was well-known. Acquainted with every inch of the Far West, and with all the Indian tribes who inhabited it, he never failed to outwit his Red enemies, and generally made his appearance at the rendezvous, from his solitary expeditions, with galore of beaver when numerous bands of trappers dropped in on foot, having been despoiled of their packs and animals by the very Indians through the midst of whom old Williams had slipped."

They called him Old Solitaire for his lonesome ways (Bill wasn't that lonesome, he always seemed to have an Indian woman waiting somewhere). Fact is, he spoke several dialects and was more at home among the friendly tribes than he was with his own people. It was said he came West as a missionary to the Osage Indians, but they converted him. He took an Osage wife and after bearing two daughters, she died. So Bill headed for the mountains and became a trapper.

Bill had more lives than a cat, surviving one hair-raising adventure after another. His luck finally ran out after some 30 years in the wilds, when on March 14, 1849, a war party of Utes killed Bill and Dr. Ben Kern near the headwaters of the Rio Grande in southern Colorado.

Two years later, Richard Kern, a brother of Dr. Kern, was traveling with the Sitgreaves Expedition in Northern Arizona. Kern took copious notes of everything he saw and heard on the journey. During the trip Kern and guide, Antoine Leroux, applied the name Bill Williams to the 9,200 foot range. Later, the pair honored ol' Bill again by giving his name to the river that headwaters near Hackberry. Later it was changed to Big Sandy. Today, the stream becomes the Bill Williams River after it joins the Santa Maria River near Alamo Lake on its journey to the Colorado River.

Like the Indians, with whom they sometimes lived with and sometimes fought, mountain men like ol' Bill were "Nature's Children." They loved the outdoors, hated fences and restrictions, respected grizzlies and rivers and rode anything that "wore hair."

Storing the knowledge of this vast *terra incognita* in their heads, they guided the storied Army Corps of Topographical Engineers on their historic surveys along the 32nd and 35th Parallels during the 1850s. These trails or paths later became the trails that led emigrants to the promised land in what has been called the greatest mass migration of greenhorns since the Children of Israel set out in search of Caanan.

Prescott's First Citizen

When old Joe Walker, a big, strapping, ex-mountain man, and his party of prospectors arrived at Granite Creek in the Spring of 1863, another old mountain man, Pauline Weaver, was already camped there. The area where the future territorial capital city of Prescott would be founded was the stomping grounds of the Yavapai and Tonto Apaches. Both groups had a reputation as formidable foes of the whites who asked no quarter and gave none. Surprisingly, the earliest days of Prescott's history were relatively free of bloodshed and the credit goes to Pauline Weaver.

Weaver is one of those ubiquitous characters who best fits the description of one who never had time to write or narrate early Arizona history—he was too busy making it. Born in Tennessee around 1800, he was the son of a white father and Cherokee mother. For a time he worked for the Hudson Bay Fur Company but preferred warmer climates, so he headed for the Southwest. He first arrived in Arizona in the late 1820s and over the next few years established a reputation as a first-rate mountain man, coming to know Arizona's mountains, deserts and rivers like the back of his hand. Somebody scratched his name on the Casa Grande ruins in 1832. Since Weaver made his mark with an "X" until his dying day, the signature is but one more mystery at that site.

During the Mexican War, General Stephen Watts Kearny, commander of the Army of the West, hired Weaver as a guide for the Mormon Battalion on its historic road building trek along the Gila Trail. Weaver spent the 1850s trapping for beaver along the river streams in Arizona where he got on friendly terms with most of the tribes.

In 1862, some natives along the Colorado River in western Arizona showed him some rich gold placers at La Paz not far from today's Ehrenberg. Before the gold played out, some 12 million dollars worth of the yellow metal had been panned out.

The boom town of La Paz that spring up nearby almost became the capital city of the Arizona territory. Sometime later the capricious Colorado changed its muddy course and left La Paz and a couple of steamboats sitting high and dry in the desert. The town picked up and moved over to the river and re-named itself Ehrenberg.

The same year Weaver discovered gold at La Paz he hired out as a scout for the California Volunteers. A small force of Confederates from Texas had occupied Tucson and were probing their way along the Gila towards the strategic river crossing at Yuma. A few weeks later they retreated back to the Old Pueblo in the face of the 2,000-man California Column that was planning to re-occupy Arizona.

The hard-riding mountain men led Captain William Calloway, and 272 men, up the Gila to the Pima Villages at today's Sacaton-Bapchule (I-10 at the Gila).

Two detachments from Calloway's Cavalry troop headed to Picacho where they fought a battle with the Confederates rear guard in what is called the "Westernmost Battle of the Civil War."

Not long after the Walker party found gold in the Bradshaw Mountains, Weaver guided the Abraham H. Peeples party up the Hassayampa River in search of another *madre del oro*. A few miles north of Wickenburg they stumbled upon a treasure trove of gold nuggets lying atop a rocky knoll that was rightfully named Rich Hill. It was the richest single placer strike in Arizona history and how it got deposited up there is still an enigma, but gold, as they say, is where you find it.

During those first months, Weaver worked tirelessly to negotiate a treaty between the native tribes and newcomers and succeeded for a spell. The Indians used the password "Paulino-Tobacco," which was to indicate to the whites they were friendly. Tobacco was a word nearly every Indian knew and understood as it was always given by whites during a parley as a token of friendship. As more whites poured in who weren't aware, or didn't care about the arrangement, the treaty became meaningless. Too many cultural differences and mutual mistrust caused the inevitable outbreak of hostilities.

In the mid-1860s, Weaver himself was jumped by a war party outside Prescott and seriously wounded. The old scout thought he was a goner and went into his "death song"—a custom he'd adopted from the Plains Indians. The suspicious warriors, not familiar with the ritual, believed he'd gone crazy and left him alone. When Weaver saw he wasn't going to die, he got up and casually walked home. The wound did, however, continue to trouble him for the remainder of his days.

It is said the natives were remorseful about shooting Weaver and during friendly parleys always asked how "Powlino" was getting along.

When the first settlers moved into the Verde Valley, the army was called in to provide protection from a growing number of attacks. The officers wisely brought Weaver in to bring about a peace treaty. His service, according to military records, was invaluable but ol' Dad Time was catching up. His health deteriorated and, on June 21, 1867, Pauline Weaver died. He was buried at Camp Verde (Lincoln) with full military honors. Later, when the post was abandoned his remains were taken to California.

In 1929, poet-historian Sharlot Hall organized a campaign to have Weaver's remains returned to Prescott. Thanks to the Boy Scouts and Prescott school children, funds were raised and Weaver was re-buried on the grounds of the old Territorial capitol. Ms. Hall declared him Prescott's First Citizen—a title he richly deserved.

Early Mormon Missions

The first Mormon colonists from Utah arrived in Arizona in early 1854. The Navajos were on the warpath at the time and the Saints were driven out a year later. Between 1858 and the early 1870s Jacob Hamblin, the Mormon's greatest trailblazer, made several reconnaissance missions, locating river crossings, water holes and suitable trails. By this time the Navajos were at peace thus making attempts at colonization safer. However, the greatest enemy facing the newcomers was the harsh, arid land and the fickle moods of the Little Colorado River.

Mormon settlements at Kanab (Utah), Pipe Springs and Lee's Ferry were designated as bases from which to launch new colonies in Arizona.

The primary mission of the Church during these years was expansion. Under the dynamic leadership of Brigham Young, the Mormons were determined to establish a far-flung empire from their Utah base west to California and south to the Salt River Valley and eventually to Mexico.

A reconnaissance expedition was sent to the Little Colorado River Valley in 1873 to make a feasibility study for colonization. The scouts reported it unsuitable. A Norwegian missionary, Andrew Amundsen, pretty well summed up the bleak land. His spelling left a little to be desired but the meaning was clear: "From the first we struck the little Colorado . . . it is the seam thing all the way, no plase fit for a humg being to dwell upon." Amundsen concluded his report rather succinctly calling it, "The moste desert lukking plase that I ever saw, Amen."

Despite this foreboding declaration, an expedition of some 100 colonists left Utah in early 1873 headed for the Little Colorado determined to make a go of it.

They arrived on the Little Colorado in late May after a miserable, wind-blown journey down Moenkopi Wash. By this time the river was drying up. One journal entry referred to the Little Colorado, disparagingly, as "a loathsome little stream. . .as disgusting a stream as there is on the continent."

Iron-willed and purposeful at the outset, the dispirited colonists soon packed their gear and returned to Utah.

Undaunted, Brigham Young was determined to establish colonies in the valley of the Little Colorado River. Three years later he tried again, this time with success.

A major figure in the Mormon colonization along the Little Colorado River was a fiery redheaded frontiersman named Lot Smith. Smith and other church leaders like William C. Allen, George Lake and Jesse D. Ballinger led parties of colonists to the lower Little Colorado River Valley to the sites of today's Joseph City, and Sunset Crossing (Winslow) and Holbrook. Town sites were marked, irrigation ditches were dug, dams erected and crops were planted. The Mormons had, at last, taken permanent root in Arizona.

The four colonizing parties, each numbering about 50, established camps and named them for their respective captains. Soon after the names were changed. Lake's Camp became Obed; Smith's Camp was changed to Sunset, for the river crossing nearby; Ballinger's Camp became Brigham City and Allen's Camp, St. Joseph. (Since St. Joseph, Missouri was also on the Santa Fe line, in 1923, St. Joseph was changed to Joseph City.)

As a precaution against Indian attacks, all four communities constructed forts of cottonwood logs and sandstone. These were self-containing units including communal mess halls and housing. The average size was about 200 feet square with walls reaching a height of seven to nine feet. Elevated guard houses stood at the corners. Each had shops, cellars, storehouses and wells in case of prolonged siege.

Sunset and Brigham City were short-lived communities located on opposite sides of the Little Colorado near the site of present day Winslow. In 1878, the two hard-luck communities were ravaged by floods which destroyed the year's crops. Obed suffered the same fate. Within a year, malaria and flooding caused the colonists to pull up stakes. However, the sturdily built sandstone fort survived and was used as a stock corral by the Hashknife Outfit until it was torn down in 1895.

St. Joseph was only one of the four communities to survive. Despite numerous crop failures and dams destroyed by the rampaging Little Colorado, the gritty colonists won their battle against the elements. Today it holds the honor of being the oldest Mormon settlement in the Little Colorado River Valley.

Territorial Political Shenanigans

Territorial citizens took great delight applying social acupuncture to local politicos. It's been said with dubious pride that Arizona had some of the finest legislators money could buy. Old timers around Jerome used to say that every time the subject of a bullion tax would come up before the legislature Henry Allen, superintendent of the United Verde Mine, would go over to the local bank, make a sizeable withdrawal and announce to everyone within earshot that he was "off to Phoenix to buy some mules and jackasses." A few days later, he would return, without livestock but by some coincidence the bill for the bullion tax would die quietly in some committee soon after.

Territorial legislators were generally long on politics and short on statesmanship. The pay wasn't much, they only met every other year and every bill they passed on was subject to review in Washington.

I reckon the most maligned of all 25 sessions was the infamous Thirteenth of 1885. Arizona was still pretty wild and woolly at the time. Geronimo and his band of rogues was scourging southern Arizona, Tombstone was just getting over the bloody feuding between Earps and the "cowboys" and the notorious Pleasant Valley War was heatin' up.

The boisterous parties and general rowdyism made a cowboy Saturday night look tame by comparison. They met in Prescott and had barely convened when a fist fight broke out between delegates Julius A. Brown and Lafayette P. Nash. Another delegate took a swing on a colleague with a monkey wrench and still another threatened a detractor with a bullwhip.

Two other antagonists decided to have a shootout but couldn't agree on weapons. The trouble started in a local watering hole when a Frenchman named Professor Arnold accused delegate Welford C. Bridwell of repudiating his heritage by legally changing his French surname. Bridwell a.k.a. Clay Beaulord—a hardbitten, ex-army scout—took exception to the professor's remarks and poked him in the nose and smashed his eyeglasses. The bloodied but proud Frenchman leaped to his feet and challenged Bridwell to a duel. Given challengees choice, Bridwell-Beauford wanted to use Colt revolvers. The fuming challenger opted for the more genteel French sabers. Since no such weapons were readily available the two decided to cool their tempers with a few glasses of Mumm's Extra Dry and the matter was soon forgotten.

The preliminaries now settled, the delegates got down to the business of politics. They had come to Prescott from the far reaches of the territory and each had some favorite sacred cow to obtain or retain for their county. The delegates from Tucson's delegation handed their representatives a satchel containing some $4,000 and said nothing short of the capital was acceptable. Willcox wanted to split off from Cochise County and form a Sierra Bonita County. The delegates from

Tombstone were equally determined to see that the county remained intact. Yuma wanted to keep the Territorial Prison and Florence wanted a bridge across the fickle Gila River. Tempe wanted a normal school and Phoenix wanted an insane asylum. Prescott, of course, wanted to keep the capital.

Tucson's delegates ran into some trouble on their way to Prescott and had to take the long way around. The Salt River was running high at Judge Hayden's ferry crossing, (Tempe) so they boarded the Southern Pacific at Maricopa and rode to Los Angeles thence back on the Santa Fe to Ashfork where they climbed on a stagecoach for the last 50 miles south to Prescott. At Hell's Canyon they encountered a blinding snowstorm so in desperation delegate Bob Leatherwood climbed on a borrowed mule and with the satchel of money, hightailed it to Prescott.

Unfortunately for Tucson, Leatherwood arrived too late. The trade-offs had been made. Prescott kept the capital; Phoenix got an insane asylum; and Tempe, a normal school. Also, Yuma retained the prison and Florence got a bridge across the Gila. The venerable Rio Gila has, however, a long history of going its own way and shortly after the structure was dedicated it changed its course and left that bridge standing by itself out there in the desert.

Willcox didn't get to form its own county but the heaviest blow fell on Pima County. Tucson didn't get the capital and as a consolation prize was awarded a university.

Indignant Tucsonians didn't accept this award with a great deal of enthusiasm. When the delegates came home they were greeted with a barrage of rotten vegetables and some sorehead threw a dead cat. But, the award for collegiate naivete goes to a prominent citizen who owned a saloon. "What do we need a university for?" he cried, "Students won't buy booze!"

In the spring of 1885 their work all done, the Thirteenth Territorial Legislature adjourned. They've been called the Bloody Thirteenth for all their donnybrookin' and the Thieving Thirteenth because they spent some $47,000 for amenities when the budget called for $4,000 and only one delegate was re-elected the next time around.

In spite of all this chicanery, the positive, lasting effects of their efforts were far reaching. Funds were allocated to build a railroad from Prescott north to the main line on the

Santa Fe and another linking Phoenix to the Southern Pacific at Maricopa. A fine mental institution was established at Phoenix. In 1891 the University of Arizona, situated on land donated by two gamblers and a saloon keeper opened its doors. Incidentally, at that time there was not a single high school in the entire territory.

In the spring of 1886, the Territorial Normal School, at Tempe, opened with 33 students. After several name changes it became Arizona State University in 1958.

The continuing issue of where to locate the "capital on wheels" was finally settled in 1889 when it was located permanently at Phoenix.

There is an old piece of Arizona folklore that historians can't prove, nor can they disprove, which perhaps explains how this happened. It seems that the evening before the final vote was to be taken, one of the honorable delegates from Yavapai county went down to pay a visit to one of the ladies of the evening. He had a glass eye, which he was quite vain about and after he blew out the lamp he placed the artificial eye in a water glass on a table by the bed. Sometime during the night his lady-friend got thirsty and swallowed the water and its contents.

The next morning when the delegate realized what transpired, vanity prevented him from attending the session and Phoenix took the capital away from Prescott by one vote.

Frank Murphy's Railroad

Graham

At the peak of its prosperity, the fabled Bradshaw Mountains of central Arizona produced a king's ransom in gold and silver. Towns and mines with picturesquely whimsical names like Bueno, Turkey Creek, Tiger, Tip Top, Oro Belle and Big Bug were peopled with boisterous devil-may-care miners aptly described as unmarried, unchurched and unwashed. Each community boasted it was built atop the *madre del oro* and its streets would soon be cobbled with golden nuggets.

In 1899, the vast riches inspired railroad entrepreneur Frank Murphy to extend his Prescott and Eastern Line from

Mayer into the heart of the great mountains. Although Murphy was warned he'd be stopped by this maze of rugged, perpendicular grades laced with canyons so steep that big horn sheep had to shut their eyes and walk sideways, he was determined to meet the challenge of the mountains. That's why it's best-remembered as Frank Murphy's Impossible Railroad.

This mighty railroad line wasn't Murphy's first challenge. A few years earlier, he built the famous Peavine from Ashfork to Phoenix, linking the capital city with the Santa Fe mainline in Northern Arizona. Later he ran a line from Prescott to Mayer. The mines in the Bradshaws were producing nearly $400,000 in gold and silver annually. Because Murphy owned mining properties in the area, he was most anxious to extend his railroad from Mayer into the mountains. Actually, the plan was two-fold. One spur would run up Big Bug Creek, between Humboldt and Mayer, to Poland (town, not the country). The other would extend along the eastern side of the Bradshaws then climb the lofty summit to Crown King.

In 1901, Murphy hired a band of strong-backed gandy dancers and steel-driving men back East and transported them out to Prescott. He paid them a dollar a day for their toil, twice the going rate. Even those top wages couldn't prevent a mass exodus of hired hands after a dynamite blast on a cut exposed a rich vein of gold. Undaunted, Murphy shipped in another load of track layers and the steel ribbons continued to inch their way up the slopes towards Poland and the rich mines at Walker.

On April 21, 1902, the spur line finally reached Poland. Murphy's gamble paid off immediately. Miners following a gold vein above Poland met another group tunneling from the other side of the mountain at Walker. The result was an 8,000-foot tunnel linking the Lynx-Walker District with the railroad at Poland. The first week, $180,000 in gold ore was hauled through the tunnel in mule-drawn ore cars to the railroad where it could be hauled to the smelter at Humboldt. Now Murphy turned his attention to the more difficult task of building a line from Mayer to Crown King.

The Crown King line stretched east from Mayer across the broad cattle country to Cordes before winding down Cedar Canyon and south into Crazy Basin. From there it was 13 treacherous miles and a 3,000-foot rise in elevation to Crown King. The grade was four percent and at Horsethief Canyon it took seven miles of track to go just two miles. The tracks had more kinks and lazy loops than a cheap lariat. On some of the tight switchbacks, the steam engine had to head up a short spur, then back uphill to the next hairpin turn before putting it in forward again.

In late October, 1903 an excursion train brought a party of Prescottonians up to behold the view. From atop the summit, they could see 50 miles off into the distance.

The new railroad brought civilization to Crown King. In its early days Crown King was pretty wild and woolly. The nearest lawman was at Prescott. Horsethief Basin, a lair for uncurried bands of outlaws during the turbulent 1880s, was a few miles south of town. Local legend has it that 17 men died with their boots on in the 1890s alone.

The years leading up to World War I were boomers for the railroad and mines in the Bradshaw Mountains, but by 1918 the ore was starting to play out and the line went into decline. The old iron-bellied locomotives, their boilers leaking steam, were hard-pressed to make the steep grade.

There's an old saying, "When the gold runs out, so do the people," and by the 1920s the impossible railroad went into decline. The last train pulled out of Crown King in November, 1926 and soon after the Santa Fe pulled up the rails. The old trestles were planked over for automobile traffic. Crown King became another of those "towns too tough to die" as Arizonans were beginning to take to the open road. It was ideally located high in the cool pines and air conditioning was still in the distant future. Phoenicians braved 29 miles of washboard road to escape the searing summer heat.

During his illustrious career in the bustling Arizona territory, Murphy engaged in a host of activities. He was the first superintendent of the rich Congress Mine. He was associated with the purchase of the legendary United Verde Mine at Jerome in the 1880s and he once owned the famous Castle Hot Springs Resort. Noted for his integrity, resourcefulness and ability, Murphy attracted substantial Eastern capital to Arizona and was one of the territory's most influential businessmen.

Frank Murphy, the visionary who brought the impossible railroad to fruition continued his entrepreneurial efforts. He spent the last years of his life developing plans to build a railroad from Arizona across Mexico and down to the Panama Canal. He died in Prescott in 1917 after a long illness.

Back When Just Getting There Was Half the Fun:
Rails, Trails and Skyways Across Arizona

Celebrating the Fourth of July in old Arizona was always a festive occasion. Rawhide-tough cowboys put on rodeos in the streets of Payson and Prescott. In boisterous mining towns such as Bisbee and Jerome, large crowds gathered to watch brawny miners engage in single-jack and double-jack drilling contests. Folks in Snowflake set a charge of dynamite beneath a huge anvil and blew it skyward. Just about every community staged a colorful parade down Main Street. The Fourth of July—a century ago—the summer of 1887 was pretty typical, except in Phoenix where something mighty important was about to happen—something that would alter the course of history for the small community of some 2,500 residents as no other in the 19th century. The railroad was coming to town!

Living in today's fast lane with super freeways and jet planes to carry us here and yonder, it's difficult to imagine anyone getting excited over the arrival of a little iron-bellied steam locomotive. That is, unless one considers the closest link with the civilized world for the residents of Phoenix was an uncomfortable stagecoach ride along a dusty 35-mile ride to Maricopa. From there one could climb aboard the Southern Pacific and travel to California or points east.

Anyone who has read Martha Summerhayes' classic, *Vanished Arizona* can't help but sense the magnitude of change in Arizona after the railroad. Her first trip into the territory came as a young army bride in August, 1874. The journey began by ship from California, around the Baja and up the Sea of Cortez to the mouth of the Colorado River, thence by steamboat up that capricious stream of ports like Yuma, Ehrenberg and Hardyville. Sleep, on that humid, mosquito ridden boat, was impossible and the food was stale. However, that ol' paddle-wheeler, with all its discomforts, seemed like a floating palace compared to the next phase of the journey. A harrowing ride in a bumpy wagon (Martha was pregnant at the time) into central Arizona followed roads that were hardly passable-most weren't even jackassable. She left Arizona after a couple of years, vowing never to return but a dozen years later Martha returned to Arizona—this time by rail. Her amazement at the amenities provided by railroad transportation paint a picture of how life in Arizona changed after the railroads arrived.

The Southern Pacific railroad stretched its steel ribbons across Arizona in the late 1870s, reaching Tucson in March, 1880. The rail station nearest Phoenix was 35 miles to the south at Maricopa. From the beginning, local citizens began clamoring for a railroad. Despite the fact that thousands of miles of track were being laid across the nation each year, seven railroad companies were organized and went broke in a 10-year period before a line was built from Maricopa to Phoenix.

During that time the stage line of Gilmer, Salisbury and Company ran a daily from Maricopa to Prescott, passing through Phoenix. A proposed railroad followed the same route, the old Woolsey Road, north to New River, then up through Black Canyon, hugging the Aqua Fria River most of the way before veering off to the territorial capital, nestled picturesquely in the Bradshaw Mountains. A tri-weekly stage also ran north to Prescott via Wickenburg.

In 1885, the 13th Territorial Legislature, much-maligned as the infamous Thieving Thirteenth for its political shenanigans and free spending, created an act that provided for a railroad line linking Phoenix to the Southern Pacific at Maricopa. The original railroad right-of-way was designed to go west of South Mountain and approach Phoenix from that direction. However, residents of Tempe put on so much pressure the line was changed. The Maricopa and Phoenix Railroad was chartered and the task of establishing grades and laying down track began in earnest on November 1, 1886. W. J. Murphy, famed as the entrepreneur who brought about the construction of the Arizona Canal, was the construction boss. Bridges for the Gila and Salt Rivers were to be built in San Francisco and shipped to the sites for final assembly.

An argument developed between the Pima Indians, who owned part of the right-of-way, and the railroad but there was no stopping the gandy dancers and graders. They trudged into the reservation despite threats from the natives and their agent Elmer Howard. Meanwhile, in Phoenix, another marvelous marvel had occurred. On December 21, 1887, gas lights were turned on for the first time. Those smoky old coal oil lamps would soon be a thing of the past.

By January 10, the construction crews reached the Gila and work on the bridge had begun. However, the trespassing issue with the Pimas hadn't been resolved and the Secretary of Interior suspended work and ordered the crews off the reservation. Negotiations with the natives lasted some six weeks before a settlement was reached. The Pimas were paid $60 to $85 per acre totaling $707 and work on the line was resumed. By the end of April, the line was extended to nine miles north of the Gila. Rumors spread that the railroad would reach Phoenix by June 1. Railroad stations were being built at Tempe and Phoenix, and a grade was already being cut at the south end of the Papago Buttes. A sense of excitement was sweeping the town. Folks rode out to the banks of the Salt near Hayden's Ferry to watch construction on the bridge. Teamsters were packing their gear and preparing to move their headquarters to some burg that was still without a railroad. Shopkeepers were pondering the cornucopia of new merchandise from eastern suppliers for their customers, and real estate developers (yes, we had 'em then, too) were eagerly getting ready to cash in on the boom.

About that time, Murphy's Law revealed itself. The construction crews ran out of track, causing a three-week delay. Finally, on June 19, 1887, a new Baldwin locomotive with "Phoenix" painted on its side chugged into Tempe.

Meanwhile, across the river in Phoenix plans were being made to welcome the railroad. Progress slowed as workers donned heavy buckskin mittens. The blazing summer sun made the rails too hot to handle. Work ground to a halt once again as enthusiastic locals held a boisterous, but premature, weekend fiesta.

On Monday, nobody showed up for work and new crews had to be hired. Finally, on July 3 the last of the rails was "laid in and tied down." Captain William Hancock, the man who surveyed the original town site 17 years earlier, drove in the last spike. The long-sought dream had come true—the railroad had, at last, arrived.

The next day, July 4, brass bands played, politicians spoke, an honor guard fired a grand salute and a gala celebration was enjoyed by the throngs that came out to whoop it up. The tremendous dust storm that swept across the valley that afternoon did little to dim the optimism of the little metropolis that had finally metroped.

After the hoopla died down that day, the engineer threw the little Baldwin into reverse and backed her all the way to Maricopa. Phoenix had joined the civilized world but still lacked a round house. A second-hand turntable was installed several months later.

With the purchase of a $3 ticket, same as the stagecoach fare, Phoenicians could now make the 2-hour and 40-minute ride to Maricopa in relative comfort—a far cry from those leather-slung cradles on wheels called stage coaches.

For nearly 40 years the Maricopa and Phoenix Railroad performed its mission admirably. Perhaps the most exciting event occurred in 1910 when the train was held up by youthful Woodson brothers. Using borrowed pistols and rented horses, they robbed the passengers of some $300 then rode out into the desert towards the Mexican border. The sheriff of Maricopa County, at the time, was Carl Hayden. Hayden quickly organized a posse and went in pursuit. He knew they wouldn't get far in the desert on horseback, so he commandeered a large touring car at Maricopa and continued the chase. There weren't any roads so the big car dodged cacti and negotiated the arroyos that slice across the Sonoran Desert. Hayden and his posse caught up with the desperados near Cucklebur. The searing desert heat had taken its toll on man and horse and the pair meekly surrendered. It was the first time in history a posse had pursued outlaws in an automobile. Sheriff Hayden's fame spread far and wide after the capture, enhancing his political fortunes. The next year he ran successfully for the single congressional seat in the new state of Arizona and the rest is, as we say, history.

The era of the Maricopa-Phoenix Railroad ended in 1926 when a new Southern Pacific mainline reached the capital. The event was the culmination of a long campaign. "Phoenix Must and Will Have a Mainline Railroad" was even a part of the masthead on the *Arizona Gazette* (now *Phoenix Gazette*) for 20 years.

Another major event in Phoenix rail history occurred in 1895 when the Santa Fe completed its line from Ashfork, Prescott to Phoenix. Historians generally regard this as the end of the frontier period in Arizona.

When Arizona became a state in 1912 the only viable means of hauling goods and people was by rail. When the horseless carriage arrived on the scene folks began clamoring for better roads. Road races between Los Angeles and Phoenix featuring such famous drivers as cigar-chomping Barney Oldfield and Louis Chevrolet were staged to promote road construction. Despite these efforts the state had less then 300 miles of paved highway in the late 1920s.

In 1944, the Federal Highway Act provided funds for an interstate highway system. These monies were used to complete the paving of U.S. 80, the old Gila Trail across southern Arizona and Route 66, the Beale Camel Road across the northern part of the state.

Historically, northern and southern Arizona were separated by rugged, mountainous terrain. A trip to Flagstaff was an all-day affair at best. U.S. 89 ran northwest to Wickenburg then up steep-sided Yarnell Hill to Prescott, north to Ashfork then east to Flagstaff. Or you could take the scenic route through Jerome and Oak Creek Canyon. The direct line to Flagstaff, I-17, was light years away; but the old Black Canyon stagecoach road could get you to Prescott if you didn't mind the dust. During the 1940s, it ran north up 27th Avenue or lateral 14, Mission Drive as it was called in those days, to New River where the pavement ended.

Back in 1947, the Trimble family packed up all their belongings in a '36 Ford and two-room trailer and headed for Ashfork via Black Canyon. Among our belongings were a couple of milk goats and several chickens which were temporarily quartered in the trailer. Our car broke down at Bumble Bee so we took up residence there for a few days while parts were sent out from Phoenix. Just north of Bumble Bee is a steep hill called Antelope. The old car couldn't muster enough horsepower to make the grade and had to be towed into Cordes for more repairs. We lived there a few more days while waiting for additional parts. The rest of the journey through Mayer and on to Prescott was uneventful. As I recall, the journey took about nine days. By the time we reached

Ashfork most of the furnishings in the trailer had been eaten by the goats. The chickens didn't fare too well either—we'd eaten them. It wasn't until 1955 that the paved highway was completed between Prescott and Cordes Junction on what was to become Interstate 17.

The air age, as far as the general public was concerned, arrived in Arizona on November 28, 1927; Phoenix and Tucson welcomed Aero Corporation of California's Standard Air Lines. Seven-passenger Forkers, with a cruising speed of 120 mph left Los Angeles at 8 a.m. and arrived at Phoenix at 1:30 p.m. Fare in those days was $32.50 one-way. The planes had few amenities; or as one pilot put it, "no water, no toilet, no food, no nuthin'." He might have added, no radio and no navigational equipment except a compass. The plane made one stop at Desert Center, California where a gas station operator had scraped out a runway next to his business. The planes could stop, let their passengers visit the restrooms and drink a cold soda pop while the attendant filled the gas tank.

The first municipal airport in Phoenix was located at 59th Avenue and Christy Road (McDowell Road). It was so far out in the boondocks, pilots frequently couldn't locate it and landed instead at fields closer to Phoenix. The old Central Field was at Central and Mohave. It later became the Phoenix Municipal Baseball Park. Another was at 24th Street and Van Buren (which seems mighty convenient in those pristine days of flying).

Construction began on an 80-acre parcel of desert land, to be called Sky Harbor, on November 16, 1921. It was dedicated on Labor Day, 1929. Sky Harbor, better known as the "Farm," was way out in the boondocks. The pavement and streetcar tracks ended at Eastlake Park on 16th Street and Washington. The rest of the trip was over what was better described as a dusty cattle trail. Despite that, 8,000 people braved the heat and dust to attend the dedication ceremonies. The biggest threat to safety didn't come from too much air traffic—cattle had to be cleared off the runway before a plane could land.

Gala celebrations marked the dedication of many airport terminals, highways and interstates in recent years; but none of these can match the impact of that July 4, 1887 when a shiny new Baldwin steam locomotive with "Phoenix" painted on its side chugged into town.

The Fabulous Lost Adams Diggings

Somewhere out in these rugged mountains, just maybe, lies the greatest lost mine of 'em all, The Lost Adams. According to legend a sheer canyon wall with a huge boulder at the base hides a narrow opening into a Z-shaped canyon, called by the Apaches, *Sno-ta-hay*. This hidden canyon opens up into a small valley with a stream running through. Beneath the floor of a burned out cabin lies several buckskin poke sacks containing millions of dollars in gold dust (at today's prices). Treasure seekers have searched in vain for over a century trying to locate the entrance to that mysterious canyon.

The story began along the Gila Trail in the mid-1860s. A freighter named Adams was camped near Gila Bend when a band of Apaches drove off his team of horses. Adams grabbed his rifle and ran off in pursuit. He eventually caught up with the animals but upon returning to camp saw that his wagon had been ransacked and burned.

Adams rode to the Pima villages on the Gila River hoping to barter for supplies. He arrived there to find a party of some 20 miners all excited over the prospects of getting rich. A young Mexican who had escaped from the Apache Indians had arrived with a tale of Apache gold. One of the youngster's ears had been twisted into a grotesque knot, a deformity that inspired the name Gotch Ear. He'd been captured as a child and grown up with the band, but then had a fight with one of the warriors and killed him. Fearing retaliation from the slain man's relatives, he'd fled. On his way to Sonora, Mexico, he met the American prospectors.

"I know a canyon where you might load a horse with gold in one day's gathering," he told them. "There are pieces as big as acorns, scattered on the ground. Above the gravel is a rock ledge holding chunks of this yellow stuff as big as a wild turkey's egg." The gold, the boy said, was located in a hidden canyon in the heart of Apacheria.

With promises of a couple of horses, a red bandana, a rifle and a hundred dollars, the argonauts persuaded Gotch Ear to lead them to the Apache treasure. Adams' timely arrival at the Pima villages provided the animals essential to make the trek. The 20 prospectors were without horses, and none were to be found among the Pimas, so he was invited to join up. Since he had lost everything in the Apache raid, he now figured to recoup some of his losses.

Adams' account of the next few days journey tells of traveling northeast from the Pima villages towards Mount Ord in the Mazatzals. From there the party headed across the rugged central mountains south of the Mogollon Rim. Finally, they approached a steep-sided cliff. When one of the miners wondered if they were going to scale the wall, Gotch Ear just smiled and said, "Wait and see." He led them around a large boulder at the foot of the wall and through a hidden *puerto,* or door, that led into a narrow Z-shaped canyon.

A short distance farther, they came to a beautiful valley threaded by a stream. At the far end of this box canyon was a waterfall.

"If you search the gravel at the water's edge," the Mexican youth advised, "you'll find the yellow metal you seek."

Soon after, the canyon walls rocked with the sound of whoopin' and hollarin' as the prospectors filled their poke sacks with golden nuggets.

Gotch Ear was rewarded generously and he rode off into

the darkness never to be seen again.

A few days later, Chief Nana and about 30 of his warriors paid a call. He told the prospectors they would be allowed to stay as long as they remained below the falls, but under no circumstances was anyone to travel any further up the canyon.

Over the next few days, the miners set up camp. Some built a log cabin, a few hunted, while the rest panned the nugget-laden stream. The gold was loaded in buckskin bags and placed in a hole beneath the cabin's hearth. When supplies ran low, a small party was sent over to Fort Wingate, New Mexico to purchase more.

Despite the stern warning of the Apache chief, a few curious prospectors climbed above the falls searching for golden boulders, "the size of wild turkeys' eggs." And they found some. One brought back a coffee pot half-filled with nuggets.

Meanwhile, the supply party was a few days late returning, so Adams and a man named Davidson went to search for them. Near the hidden entrance to the canyon, circling buzzards provided the first mute warning of tragedy. Adams and Davidson quickly buried the bodies in shallow graves and hurried back to the camp to give warning. Long before they reached the little valley, they heard the war cries of the Apaches. The wary pair crept close enough to see the bloody massacre's aftermath before making their way back through the canyon.

Several days later, an army patrol from a camp near the future site of Fort Apache discovered Adams and Davidson dazed and delirious from their tortuous ordeal. The soldiers carried them into the camp where Davidson soon died. Adams recovered and went to California. All he had to show for his efforts was a solitary gold nugget—about the size of a wild turkey's egg.

Adams returned to Arizona after the Apache wars ended and spent the rest of his life trying to relocate the Z-shaped canyon called Sno-ta-hay. His long, unsuccessful quest ended with his death at the age of 93.

Land
of the
Long Shadows

Geologists like to say this vast land of dramatic salmonhued sandstone spires was once buried 3,000 feet beneath ancient seas. Over the next several million years, layer after layer of sediments were deposited, then hardened, followed by an uplifting of the land. It's difficult to imagine, but the tops of these mountains and spires were, at one time, ground level. As the land continued to rise and the sea abated, the forces of wind, rain and time, or simply said, the rough hand of nature etched and sculpted the spectacular sandstone monoliths that we call Monument Valley.

Anthropologists generally agree that the people we call Navajo came to North America some 6,000 years ago over a land bridge on the Bering Strait. They go on to say these people drifted down from Canada and began to settle in Monument Valley about 500 years ago.

Scientifically speaking, that's how all this came to be. However, the old Navajo Medicine Man tells it another way. It is usually in the winter, when Left-Handed Wind howls fierce across *Dinetah*, that the storyteller gathers his listeners inside the confines of the hogan and tells, once again, the legend of the emergence of the people into the Glittering World.

According to Navajo legend, the people of Dinetah progressed through three previous worlds before arriving in this, the Fourth World. First World was black as there was no light from the sun, moon or stars. The creatures who inhabited First World had no form and were called Mist People.

In this mythological world, First Man and First Woman were created. Their purpose was to arrange conditions suitable for the Navajo. Unfortunately, the Beings began quarreling and began casting evil spells upon one another, so First Man, First Woman, along with the Mist People left and moved up into the Second, or Blue World.

Here they found other people and also animals including badgers, wolves, kit foxes and cougars. These animals were at war with each other. To add to the chaos, the Evil Beings from First World had also emerged into Second World. Coyote, a cunning, but sometimes mischievous critter, who always exists in these stories, persuaded the people to leave the miseries of the Blue World and move to Third World.

The Third World was called Yellow World and had two rivers. One, a female, ran north and south. The other was male and it ran east and west. First Woman was not happy with Third World and wanted the people to move on to Fourth World so she encouraged Coyote to steal Water Monster's baby knowing it would anger Water Monster. Water Monster, as expected, caused a great flood. All the people and animals climbed up and out of Yellow World and descended into the Fourth or Glittering World. Turkey was the last to escape the rising flood waters. At the last moment, the waters touched the tip of Turkey's tail feathers and that is why, to this day, the tip of the turkey's tail feathers are white.

In Fourth World the deities, called *Yay-ee-ee*, taught the people how to live in the peaceful way and First Man and First Woman taught the people how to build hogans and to bless them with white and yellow cornmeal along with pollen and powder from prayer sticks. The first hogan was supported by five forked poles, one from the north, south and west. Two poles supported the doorway which was always in the east because First Headman, who gave wisdom to the people who lived in that direction.

Day and Night, the Sun, Moon and Stars were created in Fourth World. The four sacred mountains, San Francisco, Navajo, La Plata and Blanca were created from soil carried in from Third World.

One day, First Man and First Woman found a baby girl. The child grew rapidly into the beautiful Changing Woman representing nature and the seasons. She became the most beloved of all the Holy People.

Changing Woman mated with the Sun and gave birth to The Twins. Because Fourth World was infested with terrible monsters, Changing Woman feared The Twins would be harmed. She hid them deep underground in a hole she'd dug in the hogan. Even their father, the Sun, did not know their whereabouts.

One day The Twins discovered another deep hole where they found Spider Woman. Spider Woman liked The Twins and promised to protect them from the Monsters by teaching them special prayers and chants. The Twins returned to Changing Woman and told her of the great powers given them by Spider Woman. Having no reason now to fear the monsters, Changing Woman and The Twins cast a spell on the huge beasts, turning them to stone.

Today those massive monsters stand frozen in time in Monument Valley. And, that's the way this beautiful valley and its indestructible people came into being.

The Legend of Red Ghost

Most folks will tell you camels are not found in Arizona's high country. Truth is, those adaptable beasts can thrive in just about any kind of terrain. The U.S. Army introduced camels to the Southwest back in the 1850s, using them as beasts of burden while surveying a road across northern Arizona. But, the Civil War interrupted the great camel experiment, and most of the homely critters were sold at auction. A few were turned loose to run wild—and therein lies the basis for the legend of Red Ghost.

The story begins back in 1883 at a lonely ranch near Eagle Creek in southeastern Arizona. The Apache wars were drawing to a close. However, a few renegade bands were on the prowl, keeping isolated ranches in a constant state of siege. Early one morning, two men rode out to check on the livestock leaving their wives at the ranch with the children. About midmorning, one of the women went down to the spring to fetch a bucket of water while the other remained in the house with the children.

Suddenly one of the dogs began to bark ferociously. The woman inside the house heard a terrifying scream. Looking out the window, she saw a huge, reddish-hued beast run by with a devilish-looking creature strapped on its back.

The frightened woman barricaded herself in the house and waited anxiously for the men to return. That night they found the body of the other woman, trampled to death. Next day tracks were found, cloven hoof prints much larger than those of a horse, along with long strands of reddish hair.

A few days later, a party of prospectors near Clifton were awakened by the sound of thundering hoofs and ear-piercing screams. Their tent collapsed, and the men clawed their way out of the tangle just in time to see a gigantic creature run off in the moonlight. The next day, they too, found huge clovenhoof prints and long, red strands of hair clinging to the brush.

Naturally these stories grew and were embellished by local raconteurs. One man claimed he saw the beast kill and eat a grizzly bear. Another insisted he had chased the Red Ghost, only to have it disappear before his eyes.

A few months after the incident with the miners, Cyrus

Hamblin, a rancher on the Salt River, rode up on the animal while rounding up cows. Hamblin recognized the beast as a camel, with something tied to its back that resembled the skeleton of a man. Although Hamblin had a reputation as an honest man and one not given to tall tales, many refused to believe his story. Several weeks later, over on the Verde River, the camel was spotted again, this time by another group of prospectors. They, too, saw something attached to the animal's back. Grabbing their weapons they fired at the camel but missed. The animal bolted and ran, causing a piece of the strange object to fall to the ground. What the miners saw made the hair bristle on their necks. On the ground lay a human skull with some parts of flesh and hair still attached.

A few days later, the Red Ghost struck again. This time the victims were teamsters camped beside a lonely road. They said they were awakened in the middle of the night by a loud scream. According to the terrified drivers, a creature at least 30 feet tall knocked over two freight wagons and generally raised hell with the camp. The men ran for their lives and hid in the brush. Returning the next day, they found cloven-hoof prints and red strands of hair.

About a year later, a cowboy near Phoenix came upon the Red Ghost eating grass in a corral. Traditionally, cowboys have been unable to resist the temptation to rope anything that wears hair, and this fellow was no exception. He built a fast loop in his rope and tossed it over the camel's head. Suddenly the angry beast turned and charged. The cowboy's horse tried to dodge, but to no avail. Horse and rider went down, and as the camel galloped off in a cloud of dust, the astonished cowboy recognized the skeletal remains of a man lashed to its back.

During the next few years, stories of the Red Ghost grew to legendary proportions. The creature made its last appearance nine years later in eastern Arizona. A rancher awoke one morning and saw the huge animal casually grazing in his garden. He drew a careful bead with his trusty Winchester and dropped the beast with one shot. An examination of the corpse convinced all that this was indeed the fabled Red Ghost. The animal's back was heavily scarred from rawhide strips that had been used to tie down the body of a man. Some of the leather strands had cut into the camel's flesh. But how the human body came to be attached to the back of the camel remains a cruel mystery.

The Escape of Augustine Chacon

Graham

Augustine Chacon was one of the last of the hard-riding desperados who rode the owl-hoot trail in Arizona around the turn of the century. Chacon was a resident of Sonora but did most of his mischief in Arizona, leading his gang on farflung forays of pillage and plunder. One time Chacon and his *pistoleros* robbed a stagecoach outside Phoenix. On another occasion, they held up a casino in Jerome and killed four people. After each raid, they'd hightail it back to their sanctuary in Mexico. Chacon once boasted he had 30 *gringo* notches carved on the butt of his pistol. Some say he carried much Apache blood in his veins. The bandit's undoing began after he murdered a deputy named Pablo Salcido at Morenci in 1896. Lawmen caught up with Chacon before he could reach the border and he was brought to Solomonville and tried for murder. A jury found him guilty and the notorious bandit was sentenced to hang. It looked like the end of the line for one of Arizona's most cold-blooded killers.

Augustine Chacon spent the weeks before his hanging plotting an escape. He was a tall, lean, handsome man with a thick shock of hair and a way with the women. His friends and admirers, of which there were many among the poor Mexicans living in the nearby mining camps, called him *Peludo,* or Hairy One, and saw him as a kind of frontier Robin Hood. They were eager to assist the charismatic outlaw in his getaway. A beautiful senorita-groupie inserted a hacksaw blade in the binding of a huge family Bible and smuggled it into Chacon's cell. During the next few evenings while Chacon was sawing away on the bars, the other prisoners, equipped with a guitar and concertina endeavored to play some lusty *corridos* or songs. The cacophony, or music, was intended to cover up any noise from Chacon's sawing. On the night of the escape Chacon's lady friend slipped inside the jail, batted her long eyelashes and smiled sweetly at the night guard. That was enough to lure the red-blooded deputy into the backroom for a brief, but deep and meaningful, relationship. Meanwhile, the band played on and Chacon sawed through the last bar, escaping into the night just a few days before his scheduled hanging.

Chacon continued his wild and woolly ways but his days were numbered, however, for in 1902 the newly-formed Arizona Rangers vowed to get him. Ranger Captain Burt Mossman slipped into Mexico, captured the bandito and delivered him to authorities amidst howls of protest from the Mexican government. This time Augustine Chacon was guarded closely: no saw blades inside a Bible, no mariachis and no beautiful damsel willing to relinquish her virtue on his behalf. On November 23, 1902, Augustine Chacon was hanged at Solomonville.

Charles Poston's Arizona Adventure

On the morning of March 10, 1856, Capt. Hilarion Garcia and his company of soldiers stood at attention while the tricolors of the Mexican Republic were lowered for the last time over the tiny presidio at Tucson. It had been two years since the United States had purchased the land from Mexico, but Mexican troops continued to man the small garrison. A small contingent of Americans living in the adobe community on the banks of the Santa Cruz River cheered heartily as the stars and stripes were raised. After the ceremonies, Garcia, along with his cavalry troops and their families in the wagons behind, rode south along the dusty road leading to Mexico.

Tucson, which had a population of some 1,000 during times of peace with the Apaches, had dwindled to about 350 residents due to the resumption of raiding and plundering. Early American explorers reported seeing decaying ruins of once-prosperous ranches and mines.

The wheels of bureaucracy turn slowly at times; and in spite of these Apache depredations, Tucson was without military protection from Garcia's departure in March until Major Enoch Steen and his First U.S. Dragoons arrived eight months later.

During the time between the departure of Mexican soldiers from Tucson and the arrival of the dragoons, a sizable party of American miners arrived under the leadership of an adventuresome young man named Charles Debrille Poston. They were headed for the mineral-rich Santa Rita and Cerro Colorado Mountains, south and west of the Old Pueblo. During the next few years, they would mine a fortune in silver.

Then, at last, the world heard of the bleak, isolated region people were beginning to call Arizona. Because of this new-found wealth, the United States would, in 1863, create the territory of Arizona. Charles Poston, who played a key role in opening one of the first Arizona mining operations, would also be a leading figure in the political struggle for territorial status, something that would earn for him the title, Father of Arizona. To understand fully, it is necessary to go back a few years to 1848.

When the war with Mexico ended, the United States became landlord of a vast area about which they knew very little. A primary goal in that war was to acquire California and a suitable route for a wagon road and railroad to the Pacific Ocean. The discovery of gold that same year gave added incentive.

Unfortunately, Nicolas Trist, the U.S. negotiator during the Treaty of Guadalupe Hidalgo, failed to gain a suitable right-of-way to build this all-important road to the Golden State. So in 1853, James Gadsden was sent to Mexico to purchase more land. The result was an additional 29,640 square miles. The area included all of today's Arizona south of the Gila to the international boundary. The only non-Indian communities were the small Mexican garrisons at Tucson and Tubac. The latter was practically abandoned due to Apache raidings.

The ink on the Gadsden Treaty wasn't dry when Americans began making their forays into the new acquisition. The lure of gold and silver drew would-be millionaires to the area like the mythical sirens beguiled Jason and his band of Argonauts.

It wasn't silver that first brought Poston to Arizona. Two years before the mining adventure, he had entered the new Gadsden Purchase with grand illusions of locating a railroad terminus on the Arizona "seacoast."

During the opening of new lands in the Oklahoma Territory in the early 1900s, those who entered legally— starting at the sound of the land agent's gunshot—were called Boomers. However, there were those who sneaked in early and staked out claims. These were called Sooners.

Arizona, too, had a few Sooners. One of these was Poston.

Poston was an enigma. He's been called everything from a grandiose schemer to the Prince of Pioneers. He was certainly one of Arizona's most colorful promoters.

He was an eloquent storyteller with a fertile mind; an enthusiastic visionary who was often impractical. He was also extravagant, controversial and ambitious.

He was an adventurer, explorer, author, news correspondent, miner, government official and even a poet. His checkered career ranged from plodding through the trackless wastes of the Sonora Desert on a mule to the highest inner circles of Washington politics.

He was the "Man for all Seasons" to the poor Mexican families who were in his employ at Tubac; he was also a self-indulgent, arrogant Indian agent, the first of many who would exploit the natives under his charge.

He was involved with the opening of the first American mines in Arizona and might have been a wealthy mining magnate, yet he died in poverty in Phoenix around the turn of the century.

His most notable achievement was playing a key role in the creation of the Arizona Territory in 1863. He embellished that role to a high degree in later years, falling victim to that syndrome of the "self-styled old timer." He outlived most of his contemporaries, becoming the consummate storyteller around the lobby of the old Adams Hotel.

Perhaps that is the tragedy of Charles Poston's life. Had he died bravely in battle with the Apaches—and his bravery on the Arizona frontier during those turbulent times was never questioned—he might be better-remembered. Instead, his last years were spent as a pitiful old storyteller, spinning yarns for anybody who cared to listen.

He was born on April 20, 1825, on a farm near Elizabethtown, Kentucky. When he was seven, his father, Temple Poston, moved the family to town and established a small newspaper. Young Charles spent his early years as a news carrier and printer's devil, learning something about writing along the way. When he was 12 years old, his mother passed away. His father, unable to care for the boy, apprenticed him to a wealthy Kentuckian named Samuel Haycroft; and in 1848, he married Haycroft's daughter, Margaret. But Charles Poston was restless and ambitious. He decided to seek his fortune in the Far West; and through the influence of his father-in-law, he secured a job in the customs house in San Francisco.

Poston's boss in the customs house was Thomas Butler King, who was also vice-president of the Atlantic and Pacific Railroad. It was this association that eventually brought Poston to Arizona. After the elections in 1853, both men lost their jobs. At the same time, rumors of a southern railroad across the lands recently acquired from Mexico spurred King to send Poston to the area to locate a possible right-of-way.

Acting as agent for what he called "the syndicate," Poston recruited a band of adventurers. No one knew just where the new boundaries of the Gadsden Purchase would run when the group set sail for Mexico in February 1854.

Poston was certain a seaport would be included in the Purchase and that the port would be somewhere along the Sea of Cortez coastline of northern Sonora. He also knew that a man foresighted enough to acquire land for a railroad terminus at the port would be wealthy beyond his wildest dreams.

Poston believed, wrongly, that the Gadsden Purchase would include all of Sonora. According to his calculations, the ideal site for a seaport was Guaymas.

Poston's voyage by sea was highlighted by a shipwreck off the coast of Mexico several hundred miles south of Guaymas. Poston and his band reached shore and were immediately taken into custody as *filibusteros* (land pirates). The only thing that saved the Americans from being tossed into jail by the suspicious authorities was Poston's superb gift of gab.

Mexico at that time was besieged by bands of rogues from their northern neighbor who were bent on "liberating" large areas of land in order to establish private republics. Stern-faced officials did not look kindly upon any American, legal or otherwise. After some delay, the group was released and began an adventure-filled trip overland through Sinaloa and Sonora.

Poston checked out every sizable port city along the coast and found none suitable for handling large ships. His dreams and schemes suffered another setback upon reaching Guaymas, which he described as "a miserable Mexican seaport town of about 3,500 inhabitants such as they are," not to mention the harbor which was too shallow and too small.

At the Bay of San Juan Bautista, near Hermosillo, Poston believed he had finally struck pay-dirt. The harbor was the best in the Sea of Cortez. He made an ambitious deal with five local landowners, including the governor of Sonora, where he was given power-of-attorney to deal with the railroad when it arrived. It was to be a 50-50 split of profits between Poston's "syndicate" and the Mexicans.

One can easily understand Poston's disappointment when he learned a few weeks later that the Gadsden Purchase failed to include a seaport. Undaunted, Poston, and those of his men who hadn't deserted by this time, headed for the Gadsden Purchase, this time with visions of reaping a fortune in the mineral-laden mountains. The party, which now numbered only seven, went north to the small Mexican rancheria at Sonoita, along today's international border.

At Sonoita, they encountered some Mexican miners who showed them some rich ore that assayed out to be more than 50 percent pure copper. The ore came from an outcropping several miles north at a place the Mexicans called Ajo.

After an examination of the area around Ajo, the Americans headed north across the desert towards the great bend in the Gila River. The party then followed the Gila downstream to its Junction with the Colorado River.

After crossing the river, Poston met with Major Sam Heintzelman, commander at Fort Yuma. It was a significant meeting for both. Poston showed the major some of his rich ore specimens, and the two became fast friends. One of the few amenities for an officer stationed in the Southwest was the opportunity to gain firsthand knowledge of prospective mining bonanzas. Leaving Fort Yuma, Poston traveled to San Francisco where he showed his ore specimens to some local businessmen. The result was the incorporating of Arizona's first copper mining company, the Arizona Mining and Trading Company, on March 17, 1855.

Then Poston went to Washington to raise more capital for the venture. Finding Eastern capitalists dubious, he began looking for other sources of income. By a quirk of fate, he ran into his friend Major Heintzelman who had been transferred to a military post near Cincinnati. Heintzelman introduced Poston to several eager Ohio investors, among them William and Thomas Wrightson. The result was the founding of the Sonora Exploring and Mining Company.

Heintzelman was named president; Poston, commandant and managing agent. A German mining engineer, Herman Ehrenberg, who had been one of Poston's original group of adventurers, was appointed topographical engineer and surveyor. The latter two would be headquartered at Tubac.

Poston was given $100,000 cash to fund his expedition. He also bestowed upon himself the title, Colonel, and headed for San Antonio, Texas, to enlist another armed band of adventurers. At New Braunfels, a German community near San Antonio, he recruited a number of what he termed "educated German miners." The rest of the brigade consisted of what he colorfully described as "frontiersmen (buckskin boys), who were not afraid of the devil . . . armed with Sharps rifles, Colt revolvers and the recklessness of youth."

Their journey took them through some 750 miles of country between San Antonio and El Paso occupied by the fierce Comanches. West of El Paso, they crossed into the always-dangerous Apacheria. A council was held near Santa Rita del Cobre at which Poston was able to convince the Apaches he was "a mighty big man." The Apaches agreed not to raid the Americans if the latter would not interfere with the traditional Apache forays against the Mexicans.

Poston had a large number of tin-types made of himself while in New York. He grandly presented these to the Apaches. Many years later, an old Apache woman told him that on several occasions her people had an opportunity to ambush the Colonel: but, remembering the pictures and the treaty, they let him pass unmolested.

The party traveled overland across Texas and New Mexico, arriving at Tucson in August, 1856. Among Tucson's citizens were some 30 Americans. Commenting on their moral character, Poston dryly noted, "they were not Methodist preachers."

Poston's company rested in Tucson for a couple of weeks. It was fiesta time, and the men were allowed to "attend the fiesta, confess their sins, and get acquainted with the Mexican senoritas, who flocked there in great numbers from the adjoining state of Sonora." A few weeks later, Poston established the company headquarters at the abandoned Spanish presidio at Tubac, some 45 miles south of Tucson.

The old fortress was still in pretty good shape. Most of the adobe buildings were still intact, but the doors and windows had been hauled away. Work crews were sent into the pine-studded Santa Rita Mountains to cut lumber. Corrals were rebuilt, and soon the historic old presidio was habitable once more.

A short distance to the east flowed the cool waters of the Santa Cruz River, and nearby fields provided abundant grass. As soon as word reached Sonora, large numbers of Mexicans arrived seeking employment in the reopened mines. Next, Poston purchased the 20,000-acre Arivaca Ranch on the west side of the Cerro Colorado Mountains. Old mines were reopened, and soon Tubac was a bustling little community.

Tubac, with its low-lined adobe dwellings and dusty streets, quickly took on the atmosphere of a pristine utopia. Far from cumbersome bureaucracy, cluttered cities and the influence of the Catholic church, Poston would later write:

> "We had no law but love and no occupation but labor. No government, no taxes, no public debt, no politics. It was a community in a perfect state of nature."

The young entrepreneur had a paternalistic fondness for the Mexicans, especially the women. "Sonora has always been famous for the beauty and gracefulness of its senoritas," he wrote admiringly. The gold rush had created a mass exodus of young men to California, leaving the ratio of women to men as high as 12 to one in some Sonora towns. Many of these unattached ladies headed north to the new American mining camp at Tubac. According to Poston:

> "When they could get transportation in wagons hauling provisions they came in state, others came on the hurricane deck of burros, and many came on foot. All were provided for.
> "The Mexican senoritas really had a refining influence on the frontier population. Many of them had been educated at convents, and all of them were good Catholics."

Poston seems to have missed little in his observations.

"They are exceedingly dainty in their underclothing, wear the finest linen they can afford, and spend half their lives over the washing machine."

The ladies of Sonora made a rich contribution to life in the community, not only providing companionship for the lonely miners but also assuming other responsibilities as well. Poston noted:

"The Mexican women were not by any means useless appendages in camp... they could keep house, cook some dainty dishes, wash clothes, sew, dance, and sing.

They could give a good account of themselves in men's games also.

". . . they were expert at cards and divested many a miner of his week's wages over a game of Monte."

Poston was, in effect, the mayor of Tubac. Accordingly, under Mexican custom, he was in charge of all criminal and civil affairs of the community.

"I was legally authorized to celebrate the rites of matrimony, baptize children, grant divorces, execute criminals, declare war, and perform all the functions of the ancient El Cadi (mayor) . . ."

Young couples who couldn't afford the $25 marriage fee charged by the priests in Sonora came to Tubac where Poston not only married them for free but gave them jobs. In gratitude, many Carlotta's and Carlos' were named in honor of the generous patron.

Life in Tubac went on its merry, uncomplicated way until Archbishop Jean Baptiste Lamy, of Santa Fe, sent Father Joseph Machebeuf to check out the spiritual condition of Tubac. The priest was aghast upon learning the marriages hadn't been blessed by a priest. He quickly ruled all marriages null and void. The priest told Poston:

"My young friend, I appreciate all you have done for these people, but these marriages you have celebrated are not good in the eyes of God."

Poston defended his actions, claiming that he hadn't charged the couples any money and had even given them an official-looking marriage certificate. The couples were then given a ceremonious salute called "firing off the anvil"—a homemade tribute made by detonating a charge of blasting powder held in check by a huge anvil so as not to cause any damages. Father Machebeuf must have felt persuaded by the persuasive Poston because he agreed to do some horse-trading.

The marriages would be blessed on the condition that Poston would refrain from activity customarily performed by the Church. A gala celebration was held, and the couples were reunited in marriage. Guests included all the little Carlotta's and Carlos'. According to Poston:

> ". . . it cost the company about $700 to rectify the matrimonial situation."

Poston enjoyed those halcyon days at Tubac. On Sunday mornings, he relaxed in one of the natural pools of the Santa Cruz River, smoking good cigars and reading six-month-old newspapers. Tubac had little government, few laws and no taxes. Employees were paid in company script called *boletas*. Since none of the Mexicans could read English, each boleta had a picture of a particular animal, and each animal represented a specific amount. A calf represented 25 cents, a rooster was 50 cents, and a horse was worth a dollar. Food for the hungry miners was hauled in from Sonora.

Fresh fruit came from the orchards of the nearby mission at Tumacacori. Manufactured goods were hauled from St. Louis over the old Santa Fe Trail.

One of the people hauling trade goods in from Santa Fe was Charles Trumbull Hayden, father of the late Senator Carl Hayden.

In 1857, the Heintzelman mine in the Cerro Colorado Mountains hit a rich vein that yielded $7,000 to the ton. The ore was hauled by wagon to Guaymas, then by ship to San Francisco at a hefty 50 percent profit. In the fall of that year, Poston sent a wagon train loaded with rawhide bags full of ore, a ton to the wagon, over the Santa Fe Trail to Kansas City. The ore was widely distributed, giving the Eastern United States its first look at the mineral potential of Arizona.

But the good times couldn't last forever. An expedition attempted to take Sonora in 1857. The group was cornered at Caborca and killed, but the furor over the affair caused Mexico to place an embargo on commerce. For awhile, Americans crossing into Mexico did so at great risk.

About the time tempers cooled, the Apaches went on the warpath. Up to this time, they had pretty much left the Americans alone, preferring to raid their traditional foes, the Mexicans.

However, when a group of American newcomers who were not associated with Poston's mines joined a party of Mexicans and ambushed a band of Apaches, war was declared on all Americans in the area. Then, in 1861, Cochise and his Chiricahua Apaches went on the warpath. Bands of marauding Apaches raided throughout the Santa Cruz Valley. That same year, the Civil War broke out, and the U.S. government focused its attention on more pressing matters.

Federal troops were removed from the area and Forts Buchanan and Breckinridge were abandoned. The civilian population, both Mexican and Anglo, were left to fend for themselves against hostile Apaches, Sonoran bandits and Anglo border ruffians.

Poston, complaining bitterly, later recalled:

> "The smoke of burning wheat fields could be seen up and down the Santa Cruz Valley, where the troops were in retreat destroying everything before and behind them. The Government of the United States abandoned the first settlers of Arizona to the merciless Apaches. Also, armed Mexicans in considerable numbers crossed the boundary line, declaring that the American government was broken up and they had come to take their country back again.
>
> "Even the Americans, the few Americans left in the country, were not at peace among themselves. The chances were, if you met on the road, it was to draw arms and declare whether you were for the North or the South
>
> "The Mexicans at the mines assassinated all the white men there when they were asleep, looted the place, and fled across the boundary line to Mexico."

The Apaches laid siege to Tubac and reduced it to rubble. There was nothing left for Poston to do but grab a few personal belongings and get out.

Poston left Arizona in 1862, barely escaping with his life. He headed for Washington to promote separate territorial status for the Gadsden Purchase, now being called Arizona. There, he met President Lincoln. The two met on some common ground as their fathers had been acquainted back in Kentucky.

After some political haggling and horse-trading, Arizona became a separate territory in 1863.

Once again, recognition for Poston's services proved elusive. Most of the officers appointed to the new territory were lame duck politicians—men who had not been re-elected in their home states. "Well, gentlemen," he asked the politicians indignantly, "what is to become of me?" Almost as an afterthought, Poston was appointed Superintendent of Indian Affairs, and he returned to Arizona briefly in 1864 in that capacity.

At that time, the only reservation in the territory was located at the Pima-Maricopa villages. Poston wasted no time becoming controversial. He was accused of creating confusion and hard feelings with the military by making unreasonable demands, such as demanding a large military escort for self-serving expeditions around the territory. He angered his Pima charges by failing to deliver promised goods and paying below-market prices for their grain.

By this time, the Pima people had been dealing with the whites along the Gila Trail for several years and had a thorough understanding of commerce. They accused him of selling goods to whites that were earmarked for the Pima reservation. The Army brought charges and Pima Chief Antonio Azul accused him of "cursing Indians and treating them badly."

The whole matter was dropped a few months later when Poston was named Territorial Delegate to Washington, an office he held only briefly before being replaced.

During the next few years, Poston held many low-level government jobs. He traveled a great deal but returned to Arizona often. In 1894, he wrote *Building a State in Apache Land* in which he gave his version of Arizona's frontier history.

In 1899, the territorial legislature, recognizing him as the Father of Arizona, awarded Poston the small amount of $25 a month. It was later increased to $35.

Charles Poston died on June 24, 1902, and was buried in Phoenix. Before his death, Poston had requested he be buried on Poston's Butte north of Florence on a site where he had planned to erect a temple to the sun. In 1925, a group of concerned citizens granted this request.

Society often waits until death to memorialize a person's notable achievements. Poston lies almost forgotten atop a bleak, wind-swept butte. Even in death, recognition has been elusive for the Father of Arizona.

Arizona's Earliest Yarnspinners

Most folks believe the art of pullin' legs attached to tenderfeet began with the arrival of windjammin' mountain men, prospectors and cowboys. But it seems that Arizonans have been tellin' whoppers to newcomers much earlier. Latter-day liars would be hard pressed to match the native raconteurs who greeted the Spanish explorers.

Legends of golden cities provided the inspiration for the great Coronado Expedition into this area in 1540-42. The dashing Spaniard and his hard-riding *conquistadores* rode roughshod over the local natives in their quest for the mythical golden boulders of the *madre del oro*. Naturally, the natives quickly learned that the fastest way to rid their villages of the unwanted newcomers was to direct their search elsewhere.

After Coronado overran the pueblo of Hawikuh (near today's Zuni, New Mexico), local natives told of seven cities to the northwest. Determined to follow every possible lead, Coronado sent an exploring party that led to the discovery of the Hopi villages.

The Hopi were far from thrilled by the presence of outsiders and told them to go further west where a great river flowed. Coronado's spirits were lifted. The claiming for Spain of the Northwest Passage—the legendary waterway across North America—would be a good consolation prize if the Seven Cities of Gold failed to materialize. So, another expedition was sent forth.

It was a great river alright, but it was twisting its muddy way through the grandest of canyons, a mile below. The mighty river looked to be only six inches wide from the explorers vantage point. No doubt the Spaniards gazed at the scenic wonder in wide-eyed amazement and a couple of daring adventurers even tried, unsuccessfully, to climb to the bottom.

Next Coronado turned his attention eastward. He didn't know it but the word was already out—the taller the tale, the more gullible these gold-hungry Spaniards were. Near today's Albuquerque, a native yarnspinner, nicknamed *El Turco,* (The Turk) "because he looked like one," told of a land to the east called *Quivira* where huge sailing ships with magnificent golden eagles on the bow carried people on a mighty river where also lived fish as large as horses. The common tableware of these people consisted of pure gold and silver. Bells of solid gold hung from the trees in this magical kingdom and were used to lull the people to sleep. Where was this golden paradise called Quivira? El Turco's response was a grand gesture towards West Texas.

El Turco's free-wheeling imagination devised a clever scheme intended to lure the Spaniards out into the desolate, waterless wastes of West Texas where they would surely perish. The plan almost worked. The timely arrival of precious rain was all that saved the gold seekers. El Turco paid for that tall tale with his life and the trail-weary Spaniards were beginning to doubt the existence of a fabled waterway or cities of gold.

After two years of searching, the Spanish returned to Mexico City in 1542. The chronicler for the expedition, Pedro de Castaneda, summed it up philosophically noting, "Granted they did not find the gold, at least they found a good place in which to search."

Juan de Oñate, a wealthy miner-explorer, was the next to encounter these Southwestern yarnspinners. He'd heard stories of fabulous silver mines, pearls, a great river and a lake of gold somewhere in Arizona. In 1604-05 he crossed Arizona and stopped to query some Mohave Indians along the Colorado River.

No doubt, sensing his eagerness to learn more about the area, the natives filled his ears with wondrous stories about a lake called Copalla where people wore bracelets of solid gold. Somewhere near was a rich island where a woman with huge feet ruled a colony of bald-headed men.

One place known to the Mohaves was populated by people with ears so large that several people could find shelter beneath each one; while in another, people slept underwater. By the time they began to tell about people who slept standing up or up in trees . . . a nation of people with only one foot . . . and some people who never ate but subsisted on the smell of food, the weary explorer was surely questioning the veracity of his hosts. "Save the rest for the tourists who'll be passing through here 380 years hence," he probably said to himself.

Incidentally, Oñate himself was guilty of at least one false rumor on this historic voyage. He ventured downstream to the mouth of the Colorado and proclaimed California to be an island. This myth would persist for more than a century.

Arizona's First Christmas in the Pines

The first recorded Christmas in Arizona, north of the Gila River, took place in 1853 at the foot of the snowy San Francisco Peaks. And it was a wild and woolly affair. The celebrants were the Army Corps of Topographical Engineers, their military escorts and helpers who were, at the time, mapping a future transcontinental highway and railroad line across Arizona. This region had only recently become a part of the United States and the Corps, America's frontier rendition of the astronauts, were called upon to explore and map it. The officer in charge was a quiet, reserved young man named Lieutenant Amiel Whipple. Earlier, Whipple had equipped and provisioned his men at Albuquerque and headed towards northern Arizona along the 35th parallel. By December 23 they reached the San Francisco Peaks and a heavy snowfall brought the expedition to a halt near the site of today's Flagstaff. Since the next day was Christmas Eve, Whipple decided to pause and let the bone-weary men and animals rest.

While unpacking the mules, Lieutenant John Jones discovered a supply of rum and wine cached by the men, no doubt, to gladden hearts on the long, lonesome journey. He also found a carton of fresh eggs that had somehow survived the rigorous journey. This unexpected surprise inspired the lieutenant to prepare a special Christmas eggnog. Late the following afternoon, while the cooks were preparing a Christmas meal, Jones was mixing bottles of liquid refreshment in a huge kettle hung over a hot fire. Next he stirred in the eggs, then added a few items from his own secret recipe. That evening, all hands were invited to dip their tin cups and make merry.

The next few hours were spent gathered around a campfire. "We sat in a circle," one wrote, "smoked, drank toasts and told jokes—hearts became lighter, blood ran more swiftly in veins, and all joined in a hearty songfest that echoed through ravines and mountains . . ."

The celebration was, appropriately enough, multicultural. The joyous Mexicans sang their native songs complete with whoops and howls and performed a moving pastoral. A couple of them had been captives of the Navajo and they performed dances learned during years of captivity. The Americans bellowed traditional Christmas carols learned in their youth.

Earlier, Whipple had dispensed some of the surplus gunpowder to the Mexican herders who proceeded to use it in the celebration. At first they fired pistols and rifles into the air but soon graduated to salvos, the resounding shock waves knocked clumps of snow from the pine branches. The event reached a sparkling climax with an impromptu fireworks. Someone threw a firebrand into a dry pine tree. The dead needles, rich in resin, sent flames and sparks high above the trees. Soon, every lone pine in the area was lit up like a roman candle. During the revelry, the intrepid old scout, Antoine Leroux, looked around suspiciously and declared, "What a splendid opportunity it would be for the Indians to surprise us tonight!"

Well, there were no war parties on the prod that night and after all the booze and surplus gunpowder was gone, the hearty celebrants crawled into their bedrolls to sleep it off.

According to Baldwin Mollhausen, a German artist and naturalist who chronicled the expedition, Christmas Day was "spent in perfect quiet . . ."—an euphemistic way of saying all hands were a little hungover. But they hadn't forgotten the true meaning of Christmas, for Mollhausen added poetically, "We looked up at the sublime summits of the San Francisco Mountains and needed no temple made with hands wherein to worship our Creator."

Antoine Leroux: The Man Who Matched the Mountains

Heroes of the Old West came about gaining public recognition in a variety of ways. Some, like Buffalo Bill Cody, came about it by self-promotion. Custer's greatest glory came after his death at the Little Big Horn. Jim Bridger was glorified in the dime novels of Ned Buntline. The prolific journals of Pathfinder John C. Fremont, along with florid writing of his talented wife Jessie, made Kit Carson a legend in his own lifetime. Others like Pauline Weaver, Tom Fitzpatrick and Ewing Young never got the recognition they so richly deserved. Perhaps the most deserving of them all, yet the least known in Arizona, is Antoine Leroux.

Unlike many who were recruited from the grog shops of St. Louis, Leroux was a member of an affluent French merchant family and educated in the finest St. Louis academies. But there was a sense of adventure in his blood and in 1822 he joined the storied Ashley-Henry Expedition that left St. Louis in 1822 and explored to the headwaters of the

Missouri River. The members of that expedition reads like a *Who's Who* in the frontier hall of fame including Jim Bridger, Dave Jackson, Jed Smith, Tom Fitzpatrick, Hugh Glass, Jim Kirker, "Frenchy" Sublette and Jim Clyman. It was a young bunch of adventurers, most were in their early 20s at the time.

Two years later Leroux was trapping in the Gila watershed of Arizona and New Mexico. By the time the Americans took over the region after the Mexican War ended in 1848, Leroux was considered the most experienced, competent and celebrated scout in New Mexico. One of his assistants on many expeditions during the interim years between 1830 and 1848 was Kit Carson.

Antoine Leroux's achievements in the opening of the Southwest is impressive. In 1846 he was a guide for the Mormon Battalion on their historic road-building trek from Santa Fe to California. In 1851, he led the first of several expeditions by the Army Corps of Topographical Engineers charged with locating proposed railroad routes. Of the four proposed routes (and all are still used today) Leroux was a guide on three, including the 32nd, 35th, and 38th Parallels.

During the 1851 expedition, under the leadership of Captain Lorenzo Sitgreaves, Leroux walked into an ambush near the Big Sandy River and took three arrow wounds from Yavapai warriors. It was said the humiliation of getting ambushed hurt the tough veteran of frontier warfare more than the painful Yavapai arrows.

After guiding the Sitgreaves reconnaissance party to San Diego, Leroux was hired to lead U.S. Boundary Commissioner John R. Bartlett and Lieutenant Amiel Whipple eastward across the desert to Yuma thence along the Gila River and across New Mexico to El Paso.

In early 1853, Leroux was hired by Captain John W. Gunnison to guide his ill-fated surveying expedition across central Colorado along the 38th Parallel. Since Leroux had a prior commitment to guide Lieutenant Whipple across Northern Arizona, he had to leave Gunnison in Utah. Later Gunnison was murdered by Ute Indians. Most believed the experienced Leroux could have avoided the massacre had he been present.

The Whipple party mapped a railroad route along the 35th Parallel spending Christmas camped at the foot of the San Francisco Peaks. A festive party was held that Christmas

Eve. The old scout's only recorded comment that night was, "What a splendid opportunity it would be for the Indians to surprise us tonight!"

Perhaps the most intriguing part of the Antoine Leroux story goes back some 50 years before his birth. Strangely, and ironically, it began in New Mexico where he later gained his reputation.

About 1750, a Comanche chief, named Onacama, visited Taos during a trade fair and was smitten by the beautiful four-year-old granddaughter of Don Pablo Villapando, the biggest ranchero in the valley. Onacama wanted to purchase the little girl and raise her to become one of his wives. But Don Pablo saw an opportunity to protect his ranch from frequent Comanche raids and he struck a secret bargain. "If the Comanche will cease raiding my ranch, I will let you take her for a wife when she is old enough," he told the chief.

The Comanche chief stuck by his agreement for ten years. Each year the youngster grew more beautiful. Finally, in 1760, Onacama demanded the 14-year-old girl, saying she was ready for marriage.

Fearing for his granddaughter's safety, Don Pablo took her and fled. Enraged, the chief gathered his warriors and began one of the bloodiest massacres in New Mexico history.

Onacama's warriors hit Don Pablo's ranch and killed all the men and any women who took up arms including the patron's wife Anna Maria. During the attack she bravely grabbed a lance and charged a party of warriors and was beaten to death. Among the 56 women and children taken prisoner was 34-year-old Maria Rosalia, the little girl's mother. Later, she was sold to the Pawnees where she met and fell in love with a French trader named Jean Baptiste Lalote. He took her to St. Louis where they were married and raised two daughters. One, Helene, married a French merchant named William Leroux. They had four children, the youngest, born about 1801 was named Antoine.

So Antoine's return to Santa Fe in 1824 completed the circle of a tragic incident involving his ancestors many years earlier.

Yuma's First Citizen Was A Lady

One of the most colorful ladies who ever rode the old West was Sarah Bowman of Yuma. She didn't fit the common frontier stereotype woman—calico dress, sunbonnet and a youngster hanging on each arm with another tugging at her skirt. In fact, there wasn't anything common about Sarah. They called her the Great Western, after the biggest sailing ship of her day. Since she stood 6' 2" that didn't seem to bother her; in fact, she liked the comparison.

The red-haired lady with blue eyes was a Southwestern legend in her own time. She could literally sweep men right off their feet (and did on more than one occasion). Because of her bravery during the Mexican War at the battle of Fort Texas, the soldiers affectionately dubbed her the American Maid of Orleans. The part about her being a "maid" was stretching things a bit but that happens a lot in Texas. Some folks might have questioned her morals—she had a long string of "husbands" during the war—but nobody ever questioned her bravery or generosity. During the seven-day bombardment of Fort Texas (later Fort Brown) by Mexican artillery she dodged shells to serve hot coffee and soup to soldiers. Once she joined a battle charge declaring that if someone would loan her a pair of trousers she'd whip the whole Mexican army all by herself.

Sarah Bowman was born in Clay County, Missouri in 1812 and seems to have led a rather uneventful life until the war with Mexico broke out in 1846. When her husband volunteered for service she came along as a cook and laundress. He got sick and was put in a hospital so Sarah left him behind and went on with the regiment to Fort Texas on the Rio Grande.

During the siege she and nine other women, along with 50 men, were trying to hold against a superior Mexican force until the arrival of General Zachary Taylor's army. Sarah was supposed to be sewing sandbags from soldiers tents but opted for more hazardous duty, defiantly dodging bullets to bring aid and comfort to the troops and thus earned their everlasting admiration. When Taylor's army advanced into Northern Mexico she went along setting up hostels along the way. For Sarah it was truly a labor of love. Her husband died in the fighting around Monterey but the redoubtable Great Western continued to be the belle of Taylor's army.

During the two-day battle of Buena Vista, Sarah's commanding presence caught the attention of officers and men alike as, once again, she moved fearlessly around the battleground serving hot coffee to the weary soldiers.

When the war ended, Sarah loaded her wagons and decided to ride along with Major Lawrence Graham's dragoons to California. When told army regulations required that a woman couldn't travel with the troops unless she was married to one, she gave a snappy salute and announced with great alacrity, "All right, I'll marry the whole squadron." She climbed atop the hurricane deck of her Mexican donkey and rode down the line shouting, "Who wants a wife with $15,000 and the biggest legs in Mexico! Come my beauties, don't all speak at once—who is the lucky man?"

A fella named Davis took the challenge. "I have no objections to making you my wife," he said, "If there is a clergyman here to tie the knot." "Bring your blanket to my tent tonight," she laughed, "and I will learn you a knot that will satisfy you, I reckon!"

Sarah's 'marriage' to Davis didn't last long. A short time later she cast her eyes on some mountain of a man her own size and fell madly in love—for a while. Actually, she switched husbands several times along the way.

Sarah got sidetracked in Franklin (El Paso), Texas and spent the next few months running an eating establishment that offered the customers other amenities not usually found in restaurants. Later, on the way to California, Sarah stopped at Arizona City (Yuma) at the Colorado River crossing and decided to set up business in a "dirt-roofed adobe house."

Author Raphael Pumpelly noted in 1861 that Sarah was the only resident in the eight-year-old town. He described her as ". . . no longer young" and ". . . was a character of a varied past. She had followed the war of 1848 with Mexico. Her relations with the soldiers were of two kinds. One of these does not admit of analysis; the other was angelic, for she was adored by the soldiers for her bravery in the field and for her unceasing kindness in nursing the sick and wounded . . ."

Author-adventurer Captain James Hobbs described her as, "liked universally for her kind, motherly ways . . ." during the war.

Another observer, Jeff Ake said, "She always packed two pistols, and she shore could use 'em." He went on to say admiringly, "She was a hell of a good woman." According to Ake's father, Sarah was, "The greatest whore in the West." In the proper context, this seems to be intended as a compliment.

Fort Yuma was evacuated briefly during the Confederate occupation so when the soldiers prepared to march to San Diego, Sarah sent her "girls" home to Sonora and "followed the guidon" once more. She returned a few months later with the California Column. Ol' Dad Time was catching up with the Great Western. She died in Yuma on December 22, 1866. When the fort was abandoned years later, her remains and those of other soldiers who had died at that post were taken and re-buried at the Presidio in San Francisco.

Historians have used a lot of words including generous, loyal, devoted and brave, to describe Sarah Bowman, the Great Western. The community of Yuma, however, pays her the greatest compliment. Folks down there proudly call Sarah Bowman their First Citizen.

Mogollon Monikers

Ever since man first set foot in this rugged piece of terrain known as Arizona, he has felt compelled to brand everything with a name. Inspiration for these place names came from a variety of sources—some quite obvious.

Lousy Gulch got its name after all the residents got lice. When Mormon pioneers decided to settle near a large stand of Ponderosa pines, they simply named their community Pine. Another group settled in a small valley where they found wild strawberries growing in abundance and decided to name their town Strawberry. Henry Clifton, a member of an early Indian-fighting militia, claimed that in 1864 the place was known as Wah-poo-eta for a prominent Tonto Apache chief better known to whites as Big Rump. The most obvious place name in Mogollon Rim country was bestowed when a group of settlers pulled into a little green valley and promptly named it Little Green Valley.

Sometimes names get changed in the process. Star Valley was named for old John Starr, who moved to Arizona from Oregon with his Indian wife in 1877. Apparently, the extra "r" got lost somewhere along the way.

I reckon people have been the source for most of the place names in the Rim Country. The name Mogollon is not Indian as often presumed, but comes from Juan Ignacio Flores Mogollon, governor of the Spanish province of New Mexico in the early 1700s.

Payson, the largest town in these parts, was named for Senator Louis Payson, who helped establish a post office here in 1884. Earlier names included, Long Valley, Big Valley, Green Valley and Union Park. In 1882 the first building, a stockade, was created. This historic site was located on what is today the fifth green of the Payson golf course.

Houston Mesa was named for Sam and Andrew Houston, who ran cattle here in the 1880s. Sam was killed in a freak accident. He got off his horse to tighten the cinch and flipped the stirrup over the saddle. His pistol was in a holster tied to the saddle horn, and the stirrup struck the hammer causing it to discharge. The bullet hit Sam in the leg and he bled to death before he could get to a doctor.

During the early 1880s, Isadore Christopher located the CI Ranch on the creek that bears his name. The ranch became the target of frequent attacks by Apaches. The war parties kept burning his place, but the stubborn rancher continued to rebuild. One day in 1882, he killed a large bear and nailed the hide on the side of his barn to dry. He was out hunting a few days later when a band of marauding Apaches rode in and set fire to the place. Army troops arrived on the scene and drove off the war party. When the soldiers saw that bear hide among the charred ruins of the barn they thought it was poor ol' Christopher. Legend has it they held a solemn funeral and buried the bearskin. It was such a touching funeral Christopher hated to have to break the news that his death, like Mark Twain's, was a bit exaggerated.

One of the most important military roads during the Apache Wars was the Crook Trail along the Mogollon Rim from Fort Verde to Camp Apache. The road was used primarily in the 1870s before the arrival of the railroad, but wagon ruts, and blaze marks on the ancient pine trees, are still visible in some sections today.

Martha Summerhayes, a young army bride, rode in an ambulance supply wagon over that precipitous trail in 1874.

Martha had a proper New England upbringing and found it hard to adjust to the coarse language used by the teamsters to coax their animals up the steep grade. She wrote:

"Each mule got its share of dreadful curses. I had never heard or conceived of any oaths such like those.

They made my blood fairly curdle . . . The shivers ran up and down my back, and I half expected to see those teamsters struck down by the hand of the Almighty . . . Each teamster had his own particular variety of oaths, each mule had a feminine name, and this brought the swearing down to a sort of personal basis."

Afterwards Mrs. Summerhayes had become something of a convert.

"By the time we had crossed the great Mogollon Mesa, I had become accustomed to those dreadful oaths, and learned to admire the skill, persistency and endurance shown by those rough teamsters. I actually got so far as to believe what Jack (her husband) told me about the swearing being necessary, for I saw impossible feats performed by the combination."

Anyone who's ever spit tobacco juice on a mule's behind from the seat of a wagon could have told her so.

The Rim Country's most suitable place name was inspired by a card game in 1875 between two old settlers, Marion Clark and Corydon E. Cooley. The pair decided they were living too close together and one should move. They agreed to settle the matter with a game of cards called SevenUp. On the last hand Cooley needed only a point to win. "If you can show low, you win," Clark said. Cooley drew the deuce of clubs.

"Show low, it is," he replied, and Show Low it is today.

Those Amazing Pathfinders of the Southwest

Manifest Destiny!

It was the battle cry of a young nation pulling itself up by the boot-straps and flexing its new muscles. This expansionist sentiment came into full bloom in the 1840s when Americans began to feel crowded and started to look west. The movement took on the air of a crusade to stretch the country from one shining sea to the other.

Following the war with Mexico, the immense Southwestern regions stretching all the way to the Pacific coast became possessions of the United States. Most of the land was *terra incognita* to all but a few hundred mountain men. These colorful fur trappers had explored nearly every nook and cranny of the area, but the vast knowledge was stored in their heads.

The new landlords wanted the land surveyed and charted, and that responsibility fell to a rugged, elite group of officers called the Army Corps of Topographical Engineers. This crack outfit of scientist-soldiers was a separate unit for only 23 years; but in that short time, they explored, surveyed and charted, gathering as much information as Spanish missionaries and explorers had accumulated in two centuries.

Their heyday was that decade of wonder and discovery just prior to the Civil War. Filling their ranks with the top graduates from West Point, the Corps combined the romance of the mountain men and the scientific prowess of the Renaissance man. They endured death, hardships, blizzards, frozen mountain passes, hot deserts and hostile tribes to blaze trails across the land for wagons and railroads to follow. Their achievements, however, have been overshadowed in history books by the California gold rush and political events leading up to the Civil War

The Corps never numbered more than 30. Decked out in distinctive blue flannel shirts, dark pants, wide-brimmed, white hats and boots, they cut a daring figure sitting on a horse or mule. Along with their scientific equipment, each carried a Sharps carbine and Colt revolver.

Accompanying these expeditions were some of the great artists of that time. Their memorable paintings evoked the grandeur of the pristine landscape. More important, they painted the natives in their pride and splendor.

In those days before specialization, these young engineers were required to have a working knowledge of botany, ethnology, geology, ornithology, meteorology and anthropology. They charted and recorded both the animate and inanimate in their notebooks and scratch pads. Laboring largely in obscurity, these naturalist-explorers are memorialized today mostly in museums and college textbooks. Perhaps the greatest of them was William Emory.

The scion of a distinguished Maryland family, Emory attended West Point where his gallant manner and zealous determination earned the slender, redheaded warrior the nickname, Bold Emory. After graduation, he was assigned to the artillery for a time, but then switched to the Army Corps of Topographical Engineers.

During the war with Mexico, Emory was assigned to head a small detachment of engineers to accompany General Stephen Watts Kearny. Kearny's Army of the West was ordered to cross the Southwest's deserts and take New Mexico and California. The Army of the West marched in and took the historic city of Santa Fe without firing a single shot.

Kearny then took a small part of his force and headed out across the trackless desert for California. They followed the Gila River across Arizona, then rode across the deserts of Southern California without incident. A few miles from San Diego, on a rainy December morning, they met a large body of Californians mounted on fine horses and armed with 12-foot lances. Bone-weary and saddle sore, the U.S. forces took a severe beating at the hands of the Californians, and Bold Emory was a hero at the so-called Battle of San Pascual. During intense hand-to-hand fighting with the Californians, he saved the wounded general's life by shielding him from an enemy lance.

The important scientific data Emory gathered while exploring the Southwest outweighed his bravery in battle. His report, *The Notes of a Military Reconnaissance*, submitted to Congress at the war's end, provided the first reliable volume of scientific knowledge about the region.

Emory also provided the nation with its first accurate map of the region along with detailed descriptions of the natural resources, flora, fauna and native inhabitants. These pioneering studies earned him a place in the most respected scientific circles of the world. Emory's *Notes* have stood the test of time and are still one of the most important primary sources of reading for students of Arizona history.

To the common observer and weary soldier, the land seemed a harsh, inhospitable, trackless waste. Emory's appreciative eyes saw it in amazed wonder. His own words perhaps best set the proper tone. He described the Gila River area as presenting:

> ". . . an inhospitable look, the mountains of trap, granite, and red sandstone, in irregular and confused strata, but generally dipping sharply to the south, cluster close together; and one ignorant of the ground could not tell from what direction the river came, or in what direction it flowed onwards to its mouth. The valley, not more than 300 feet from base to base of these perpendicular mountains, is deep, and well grown with willow, cottonwood, and mesquite."

At the river junction with the San Pedro River, he describes the valley as:

". . . quite wide, and is covered with a dense growth of mesquite, (acacia prosopis), cottonwood, and willow, through which it is hard to move without being unhorsed. The whole appearance gave great promise, but a near approach exhibited the San Pedro, an insignificant stream, a few yards wide, and only a foot deep."

The rough, mountainous terrain took its toll on the pack animals:

"Except a few saddle mules, the private property of the officers, which have been allowed to run loose, every animal in camp is covered with patches, scars, and sores, made by the packs in the unequal motion caused by the ascent and descent of steep hills."

Emory continued his perceptive observations at the site of a prehistoric Indian village:

"In the sandy arroyos where our fires burn, that look as if they had been formed but a year or two since, was broken pottery, and the remains of a large building, similar in form, substance and apparent antiquity to those so often described. Strolling over the hills alone, in pursuit of seed and geological specimens my thoughts went back to the States, and when I turned from my momentary aberrations, I was struck most forcibly with the fact that not one object in the whole view, animal, vegetable, or mineral, had anything in common with the products of any State of the Union, with the single exception of the cotton-wood, which is found in the western States, and seems to grow wherever water flows from the vertebral range of mountains of North America; this tree was found growing near the summit of the Piñon Lane range of mountains; indeed, always where a ravine had its origin."

Emory also provided the first scientific observations on the geological formations and mineral potential of the lands that would become Arizona.

"Nearly opposite our camp of this date, and about one-third the distance up the hill there crops out ore of copper and iron, easily worked, the carbonate of lime and calcareous spar. A continuation of the vein of ore was found on the side where we encamped, and a large knoll strewed with what the Spaniards call 'guia' the English of which is 'guide to gold'. . . Our camp was on a flat, sandy plain, of small extend, at the mouth of a dry creek, with deep washed banks, giving the appearance of containing at times a rapid and powerful steam, although no water was visible in the bed. At the junction, a clear, pure stream *flowed from under the sand. From the many indications of gold and copper ore at this place, I have named it Mineral Creek; and I doubt not a few years will see flat-boats descending the river from this point to its mouth, freighted with its precious ores."*

He was off a little on the last point although many emigrants to California during the next few years did float part of the way to Yuma on small rafts. Legend has it, the first Anglo baby born in Arizona came into this world floating down the Gila on a raft.

The expedition encountered bands of Apaches in the mountainous Gila country. These sturdy warriors had been at war with Mexico for many years and had fought fiercely with American fur trappers in the 1820s and '30s. Their first meetings with Kearny's army were apprehensive. Emory describes one such encounter when a band came in to trade:

"Our visitors today presented the same motley group we have always found the Apaches. Amongst them was a middle-aged woman, whose garrulity and interference in every trade was the annoyance of Major Swords, who had charge of the trading, but the amusement of the bystanders.

"She had on a gauze-like dress, trimmed with the richest and most costly Brussels lace, pillaged no doubt from some fandango-going belle of Sonora; she straddled a fine grey horse, and whenever her blanket dropped from her shoulders, her tawny form could be seen through the transparent gauze. After she had sold her mule, she was anxious to sell her horse, and careened about to show his qualities. At one time she charged at full speed up a steep hill. In this, the fastenings of her dress broke, and her bare back was exposed to the crowd, who ungallantly raised a shout of laughter.

"Nothing daunted, she wheeled short round with surprising dexterity, and seeing the mischief done, coolly slipped the dress from her arms and tucked it between the seat and the saddle. In this state of nudity she rode through camp, from fire to fire, until, at last, attaining the object of her ambition, a soldier's red flannel shirt, she made her adieu in that new costume."

Leaving the mountain country with its lush stands of grama grass, the expedition entered the desert country. Passing through deserted prehistoric villages, Emory noted the vague outlines of old irrigation ditches, remains of dwellings and pottery strewn about, remnants of an advanced civilization that seemingly had vanished into thin air. Further downstream, near today's Sacaton, they encountered a scout from the friendly Pima villages.

"Turning from the ruins towards the Pima's village, we urged our guide to go fast, as we wished to see as much of his people as the day would permit. He was on foot, but led at a pace which kept our mules in a trot.

"We came in at the back of the settlement of Pima's (sic) Indians, and found our troops encamped in a corn field, from which the grain had been gathered. We were at once impressed with the beauty, order, and disposition of the arrangements for irrigating and draining the land. Corn, wheat, and cotton are the crops of this peaceful and intelligent race of people. All the crops have been gathered in, and the stubbles show they have been luxuriant. The cotton has been picked, and stacked for drying on the tops of sheds. The fields are sub-divided, by ridges of earth, into rectangles of about 200 x 100 feet for the convenience of irrigating. The fences are of sticks, wattled with willow and mesquite, and in this particular set of example of economy in agriculture worthy to be followed by the Mexicans, who never use fences at all. The houses of the people are mere sheds, thatched with willow and corn stalks.

"With the exception of the chief, Antonio Llunas, who was clad in cast off Mexican toggery, the dress of the men consisted of a cotton serape of domestic manufacture, and a breech cloth. Their hair was very long, and clubbed up. The women wore nothing but the serape pinned about the loins, after the fashion of Persko's Indian woman on the east side of the Capital, though not quite so low.

"The camp was soon filled with men, women, and children, each with a basket of corn, frijoles, or meal, for traffic. Many had jars of the molasses expressed from the fruit of the Cereus giganteus. Beads, red cloth, white domestic, and blankets were the articles demanded in exchange. Major Swords, who had charge of the trading duty, pitched a temporary awning, under which to conduct the business, which had scarcely commenced before this place formed a perfect menagerie, into which crowded, with eager eyes, Pimas, Maricopas, Mexicans, French, Dutch, English and Americans. As I passed on to take a peep at the scene, naked arms, hands and legs protruded from the awning. Inside there was no room for bodies, but many heads had clustered into a very small space, filled with different tongues and nations. The trade went merrily on, and the conclusion of each bargain was announced by a grunt and a joke, sometimes at the expense of the quartermaster, but oftener at that of the Pima's . . .

"In the houses were stored water melons, pumpkins, beans, corn, and wheat, the three last articles generally in large baskets; sometimes the corn was in baskets covered with earth, and placed on the tops of the domes. A few chickens and dogs were seen, but no other domestic animals, except horses, mules, and oxen. Their implements of husbandry were the axe (of steel, wooden hoes, shovels, and harrows. The soil is so easily pulverized as to make the plough unnecessary.

"A woman was seated on the ground under the shade of one of the cotton sheds. Her left leg was tucked under her seat and her foot turned sole upwards; between her big toe and the next, was a spindle about 18 inches long, with a single fly of four or six inches. Ever and anon, she gave it a twist in a dexterous manner, and at its end was drawn a coarse cotton thread. This was their spinning jenny. Led on by this primitive display, I asked for their loom by pointing to the thread and then to the blanket girded about the woman's loins. A fellow stretched in the dust, sunning himself, rode up leisurely and untied a bundle which I had supposed to be a bow and arrow. This little package, with four stakes in the ground, was the loom. He stretched his cloth and commenced the process of weaving . . ."

William Emory was chosen to serve as boundary commissioner when the war ended. He would have had to resign his military commission, so he refused the offer; but he was assigned as chief astronomer for the commission. During the next six years, Emory played a prominent role in marking the 1,500-mile border between the United States and Mexico, this nation's last unresolved boundary.

A serious bone of contention among the U.S. Boundary Commission was that the military was placed under the command of a civilian, John Russell Bartlett. Bartlett, a Rhode Island scholar, was a political appointee and had no practical experience with boundary surveys.

This so-called "Puritan on the Border" wasn't much better at dealing with the Mexican boundary commissioner, General Pedro Garcia Conde. When the skillful Mexican engineer persuaded Bartlett to cede a vast amount of the Mesilla Valley back to Mexico, Emory was furious. Having crossed with Kearny's dragoons in 1846, he knew firsthand the area in dispute was the only suitable place to build a transcontinental railroad to Southern California. Bartlett, who spent most of his tenure as boundary commissioner taking expensive junkets and gathering information for a book, was finally removed. Bartlett's commission died a natural death, and the boundary dispute went unresolved.

Feelings were so strong that New Mexico Governor William Carr Lane organized the territorial militia and sent them to the Mesilla Valley. Mexican President Santa Anna countered by ordering several hundred troops into the same area. It began to look like the United States and Mexico were about to restart the war.

But neither side wanted war. There had been too much opposition among Northerners to the last one for President Franklin Pierce to risk another. Santa Anna knew Mexico could not stand another war. But he did need pesos to bolster his shaky regime and the incorrigible despot was open for bids.

James Gadsden, a railroad magnate from South Carolina, was sent to Mexico to negotiate another treaty and resolve the boundary dispute once and for all. He had five options in his diplomatic repertoire—each for a different quantity of land. The largest offer was 40 million dollars for a big chunk of northern Mexico that included Baja, California. The sums and land areas gradually dwindled down to 15 million dollars, all of which provided a port on the Sea of Cortez (Gulf of California) for Arizona.

Santa Anna would have sold the whole thing for the right price, but other influential Mexicans sought to minimize the size of the purchase, and they lobbied in the U.S. Congress toward this end. Thus allied with northern politicians who did not want to increase the size of the United States south of the Mason-Dixon line any more than necessary, the size of the purchase was cut back considerably. In the end, Congress paid 10 million dollars for 29,640 square miles. The continental United States had taken its final shape and Arizona didn't get a seaport.

By this time, Emory was recognized as the foremost authority on the 1,500-mile U.S.-Mexico border and was picked to re-draw the line. Although Northerners scoffed at the new acquisition, inside its proposed boundaries were immensely rich, undeveloped deposits of gold, silver and copper not to mention fertile agricultural lands. This was the same region that famed mountain man, Kit Carson, had testified before Congress was "so worthless it wouldn't feed a wolf."

With Bartlett out of the picture, surveying the new boundary was a lot easier. Emory and his competent Mexican counterpart, Jose Salazar Larrengui, were given the authority to determine the site where the line should run. The two parties worked quickly and efficiently with no major quarrels. The fact that the treaty stipulated that the final three-million dollar payment on the deal would not be paid until the boundary work was completed, no doubt discouraged Santa Anna from interfering with the engineers.

By October 1855, the survey was completed. The following March, Captain Hilarion Garcia gathered his troops and vacated Tucson. On November 14, 1856, the First U.S. Dragoons under Major Enoch Steen arrived in Tucson and raised the American flag.

The land south of the Gila River that opponents of the Gadsden Purchase had referred to as useless turned out to be a veritable mother lode of gold, silver and copper. Within its boundaries are some of America's most scenic mountains and deserts, and it is among the nation's richest agricultural regions. Cattle grow sleek and fat on its lush, nutritious native grasses.

It works out to have cost 53 cents an acre, which has to be one of this nation's greatest real estate bargains.

The Legend of the Bill Smith Gang

Everybody's heard of the James gang, Younger brothers and the Daltons. Their nefarious exploits have been the subject of many a sagebrush saga. What's in a name? Any hard-riding hero who had the good fortune to have a natural born handle like Wyatt, Hickock or Cody pinned on him had a big advantage on someone named Smith. Anyone who ever went out to Hollywood with a name like Marion Morrison or Leonard Slye knows the bodacious value of taking a pseudonym like John Wayne or Roy Rogers. Few gunslingers in the old West were visionary enough to picture their name on a theater marquee 40 years later, otherwise they might have done the same as the Hollywood shooting stars.

Speaking of movies, Butch Cassidy and the Sundance Kid are believed to be the only outlaws who actually saw themselves portrayed in a motion picture. It happened when they stopped off in New York City on their way to South America. They also had the dubious distinction of seeing themselves gunned down by a posse. It must have been rather disturbing to hear the audience cheer their demise. Incidentally, their real names were Robert Leroy Parker and Harry Longabaugh.

The Bill Smith gang was one of the meanest band of desperados that ever rode the owl-hoot trails of Arizona and New Mexico. Hollywood overlooked them and I reckon the name had something to do with it. So, I'd like to bend yer ear a while and tell a story about Smith and his wild bunch.

Captain Burt Mossman, of the Arizona Rangers, knew Smith about as well as anyone and according to him the outlaw chieftain had once been an honest cowpuncher who'd gone bad. According to Cap Mossman, nobody seemed to know why Smith turned his back on the law. Something he didn't spurn, as we shall see, was the chivalrous cowboy code of honor. He stood about six feet tall with a slender, muscular frame with dark eyes and thick, coarse hair. The only flaw in his handsome features was a gap between his two front teeth. He was about 35 years old when he decided to turn outlaw. The ex-cowpuncher gathered around him a band that included three brothers and four other fearless border hombres.

During the winter of 1900, the Bill Smith gang terrorized southwestern New Mexico, holding up travelers, and robbing stores. The brazen outlaws raided ranches and rustled livestock in broad daylight. Their fame spread far and wide. Before long, they were being accused of every killing and foul deed that occurred in the territory.

Finally, in desperation the citizens of southwest New Mexico grew weary of lawful efforts to apprehend the gang and formed a vigilante committee that numbered several hundred (New Mexico didn't have a territorial ranger force until 1905.) The man-hunters were in the saddle constantly scouring the rugged country along the Arizona-New Mexico line. Persistence paid off as the relentless pressure soon drove the lawless bunch into Arizona. A new base of operations was set up in the remote Blue River country along the eastern border.

When word spread that the Smith gang was now operating in eastern Arizona, Mossman dispatched four Rangers to the White Mountain area.

In early October, members of the gang were seen around Springerville. According to informants they had robbed a Union Pacific train in Utah. On the way back to their lair on the Blue River, they stole a bunch of horses.

Rangers Carlos Tafolla and Duane Hamblin of St. Johns, along with Apache County Sheriff's Deputy Will Maxwell and three others, went out in pursuit.

Despite a raging snowstorm that buried the White Mountains under a thick white blanket, Tafolla and Maxwell picked up the outlaw's trail. Realizing they might lose the trail if they went back to get the rest of the posse, the two lawmen decided to take the band alone. They were attempting to sneak up on the camp when one of the horses snorted and turned towards the pursuers. The surprised outlaws quickly reacted and dove for cover.

The two lawmen found themselves caught out in the open looking down the rifle barrels of seven desperate men not over 40 feet away. Tafolla, a cool hombre under pressure if there ever was one, called out:

> "Bill Smith, we arrest you in the name of the law
> and the territory of Arizona, and call upon you and
> your companions to lay down your arms."

Those were brave words considering the odds and the

advantage but the Ranger was determined to play out his hand. Smith and Tafolla had known each other from the early days when they were both cowpunchers. Smith called out:

> "Tafolla, we know each other pretty well. We have spent many an hour of weary toil and hardships together. I liked you then and I like you now. For your own sake, for the sake of your wife and your babies, I would spare you now. I would also spare your companion. Give me the benefit of one day and I will leave here and never trouble this country again. But do not try to take me, for by God I will never be taken-neither I, nor any member of my party."

The fearless Ranger glared back at the outlaw chief:

> "Bill, this friendship between you and me is a thing of the past. As for sparing our lives we may thank you for that and no more. For 30 days we've followed you, half starved and half frozen. Now we stand together or fall together. The only request I have to make of you-and I make that for old time's sake-is: if Maxwell and I shall forfeit our lives here, you will send to Captain Mossman the news and manner of our death. Let him know that neither he, nor the other members of the force, need feel ashamed of the manner in which we laid down our lives on this spot this day."

The knightly parley was over. A furious fusillade of gunfire echoed through that snowy basin and when the smoke lifted, the two lawmen lay dead in the snow. Tafolla and Maxwell were game to the end. Each had emptied their Winchesters before cashing in. Smith and one other outlaw had gunshot wounds. Captain Mossman was at Solomonville when word arrived of the deaths of the two brave lawmen. He quickly organized a posse and recruited two Apache trackers from San Carlos. They picked up the trail and followed it until another blizzard obliterated the tracks. Since the outlaws were the only survivors that day and they made a getaway, how did the Rangers learn the details of the fight and the chivalrous manner in which Carlos Tafolla and Will Maxwell died? Well, it was like Cap Mossman said, Bill Smith turned his back on society and became one of the most ruthless desperados of his time. Yet, in spite of that, he maintained an honorable code that bonded men of the old West. True to his word, Bill Smith wrote a letter to the Arizona Rangers detailing those last brief moments in the lives of two brave men. I reckon Hollywood let a good story get away.

Desert Ordeal

Regarding monuments Will Rogers used to say: "You don't need much monument if the cause is good. It's only the monument that's for no reason at all that has to be big."

On the outskirts of Casa Grande, along what used to be the main highway between Tucson and Phoenix, stands a simple, concrete monument surrounded by weeds and showing the ravages of the passage of time. It was erected to honor a campsite of the Mormon Battalion on December 20, 1846. Monuments like these are scattered along the old Gila Trail. Some are erected by Boy Scout troops, others by interested civic groups or the descendants of the Mormon Battalion. Some members of this famed group of trail-blazers returned to Arizona by way of Utah more than 30 years after the war to take root in the land and build a new life.

The 397 men and five women, who left Santa Fe on October 19, 1846 to mark an overland road to California, were embarking on the second half of a 2,000-mile journey, the longest infantry march in American history. It was also the roughest, requiring great stamina and rugged determination. Their commanding officer, Captain Philip St. George Cooke and guides Antoine Leroux, Pauline Weaver and Baptiste Charbonneau were trail-toughened veterans used to the forbidding rough-hewn mountains and waterless wastes laced by impenetrable, boulder-choked canyons. But the Mormons, recruited by church leaders, were unprepared for the trials and tribulations that lay ahead. They were in the army as volunteers to show patriotism and receive government-paid transportation to California where they hoped to locate a new home for their displaced church. But they rose to the occasion and their heroic achievement won the everlasting respect of Captain Cooke, the no-nonsense, professional soldier who was charged with the inglorious job of building a wagon road to California.

Captain Cooke, disappointed at not receiving a combat command, would never know that his achievements and those of his Mormon volunteers would have greater significance than any glorious charge he might have led on the field of battle. The task of building a wagon road would have been demanding enough for these citizen-soldiers: but the hardships endured along the desert trail north of Tucson, as recorded in the journals of Captain Cooke and Sgt. Daniel Tyler, paint a vivid picture of their desert ordeal. The Mormon Battalion left Tucson on the morning of December 18 following the Santa Cruz River northwest towards the Gila. Seven miles north of town the river disappeared in the sand. The mules were watered and the expedition set out across the desert cutting its way on a 24-mile path through dense mesquite thickets. At about nine o'clock that evening, they made dry camp. Sergeant Tyler of Company C, and a stake patriarch in the Church, recorded the ordeal of that first night after leaving Tucson:

> "Struggling, worn out, famishing men came into camp at all hours of the night, and the rear guard did not reach camp until near daylight."

Resuming the march the next morning at sunrise they traveled 14 miles to a place where there was supposed to be water; but when they arrived, the hole was dry. Cooke wrote:

> "There was nothing to do, but march on; there was the same baked-clay surface, with a little sand. At sundown a very small pool was come to; too shallow for dipping with a cup, but enough for most of the men to get a drink by lying down."

There was, according to Tyler:

> ". . .water enough to give the most of those present a drink by lying down to it, which was the only method allowed. Dipping was forbidden, in order that as many as possible might have a chance to drink. The main portion of the army, however, had no water during the entire day, save a few drops which the men managed to suck from the mud in small puddle holes found by the wayside."

Later that evening the pack mules were turned loose. Their keen instincts drove them to a small pool and they plunged headlong into the water. By the time the thirsty soldiers arrived it was either consumed or undrinkable. Knowing the only chance for survival was to press on, Cooke urged them to move forward. By this time the battalion was strung out across the desert for several miles. Lieutenant George Rosecrans, of C Company, rode into the hills and located a small spring where a few were able to fill their canteens.

The soldiers continued on, crossing rocky arroyos and dense mesquite thickets. Finally, Cooke called a halt to the march:

> "The battalion had then marched 26 hours of the last 36; they were almost barefooted, carried their muskets and knapsacks; the mules had worked 47 miles without water. A little wheat was now given to them."

On the morning of the 20th, the scouts left long before sun-up and were several miles down the trail by the time the battalion resumed its march. Before noon on the 20th, water was found and canteens were filled and loaded on pack mules and rushed back down the trail to assist stragglers, many of whom were now lying along the trail unable to continue.

Cooke wrote:

> "I have been mounted 32 of the last 52 hours; and what with midnight conferences, alarms and marches, have had little rest for five days . . .
>
> "The battalion have marched 62 miles from Tucson, in about 51 hours; no ration of meat was issued yesterday."

It was through the heroic efforts of those men and women, not to mention the pack mules, that the Mormon Battalion reached this little site north of Casa Grande on the evening of December 20, 1846. Will Rogers was right, you don't need much of a monument if the cause is good. This one honors more than just a campsite—it is a testament to courage, perseverance and honest determination.

People ask, "Marshall, where do you come up with those story ideas?" I usually reply, "Well, one just pops into my mind and there's nothin' there to stop it." This one just popped into my mind one day as I was driving that stretch of road that leads into Casa Grande. It sure taught me something about respect for unpretentious little monuments standing in patches of weeds beside highways.

Hohokam:
The First Phoenicians

One day back in 1867, a big strapping, energetic man named Jack Swilling was riding across the Salt River Valley bound for the mining camps in the Bradshaw Mountains. Swilling, erstwhile Confederate officer, Indian fighter and prospector, was a restless adventurer, with a past as colorful as a Navajo blanket. He sported a drooping mustache and shoulder-length red hair, in the flamboyant style of frontier gunfighters. He still carried a bullet in his side from a gunfight and a permanent headache after some adversary had crowned him with the barrel of a six-shooter. He mixed laudanum with alcohol to kill the incessant pain and was, at times, a little crazy.

Swilling was also a man of vision and an entrepreneur. He gazed out across the sprawling Salt River at the decayed mud ruins of the ancient civilization that once dwelled here. Scanning the natural contours of the land, he noticed the remains of an intricate system of canals and irrigation ditches. It was plain to see the land had once supported a large population. The canals and ditches extended out several miles from both sides of the river. He declared that if Indians had successfully farmed this valley, it could be done again. Swilling wasn't the first to see the remnants of the prehistoric dwellers and it's unlikely he spent much time pondering the wherefores and whys of this mysterious civilization. The past had inspired a vision, but Swilling was more interested in the present—and the future. Others would come later and attempt to sort out these traces from the past.

A few weeks later, Swilling returned to the Salt River Valley with 16 companions and began clearing dirt and debris from the canals and ditches. They planted wheat and barley and by the spring of 1868 the population had grown to 50.

Like Swilling, few, if any, of these 19th-century settlers gave thought to the ancient civilization that had once dwelled here. They plowed their fields and irrigated their crops. Their farming tools frequently uncovered pottery and other ancient artifacts which were casually cast aside or destroyed. Interestingly, they did recognize the pre-historic dwellers when it came time to give the settlement a name.

Swilling suggested the name, Phoenix, for the mythical Egyptian bird who, every half millennia, was consumed in flames only to emerge from its own funeral pyre—reborn with youthful vitality. A great new city, he proposed, would rise upon the ashes of an old. The local folks seemed to like the analogy and the rest is, shall we say, history. Many accounts recognize "Lord" Darrel Duppa, another resident at the time, with naming Phoenix. Both were colorful and were well acquainted. As for which one came up with the name, take your pick.

Eventually others did come to attempt to unlock the mysteries of those pre-historic Master Farmers—the ones we now call the *Hohokam*—a Pima Indian word meaning: "those who have gone," "vanished" or literally "all used up."

"How could a primitive people," archaeologists ask, "carve out an existence, develop a society and build monumental structures in such a harsh environment?"

In all, only the most durable artifacts survived—a few tantalizing clues, limiting the scope of our knowledge considerably. The Hohokam left no written record so we don't know how they governed, what they called themselves, the language spoken or what they thought. They were not as advanced as the Aztecs or Mayans but were likely the most progressive peoples in what is today's United States. Unfortunately, only a fractional amount of a cultural record has been found and recorded.

Then, who were these remarkable people who, during their peak, numbered some 20,000 in the Salt River Valley before going into a mysterious rapid decline?

Most scientists believe the Hohokam arrived in Arizona from Mexico around 300 B.C. Apparently, they arrived with a strong culture intact and had an immediate influence on the area and the people already living here. In time their influence would be felt as far west as the Colorado River, to the east, New Mexico and north to the Flagstaff area.

The 13,000 square-mile watershed above the Salt River provided a reliable water supply. During normal years, the river was probably a hundred feet wide and five to six feet deep. The banks were held in check by tall stands of willow and cottonwood trees. Digging by hand without beasts of burden (the Spanish didn't introduce oxen, horses or mules until the 16th-century) they engineered the largest prehistoric irrigation project in North America. Some of these were 30 to 40 feet wide and 15 feet deep. For construction tools they used digging sticks and stone hoes. Large woven baskets were used to haul dirt. It's been estimated 50 men and women could dig about three feet a day. More than 250 miles of gravity-fed canals were in the Salt River Valley alone.

Twentieth century engineers have marveled at the masterfully designed canals. During construction of the Grand Canal, surveyors followed a prehistoric ditch and couldn't improve on the grade. Other modern day canals also follow the grade set centuries ago by prehistoric engineers using primitive instruments.

Their main crops were corn, beans, squash, tobacco and cotton. They introduced the latter into today's United States and produced fabric textiles. Unfortunately, few examples have withstood the passage of time.

The Hohokam lived in pit houses during most of their 1700-year existence. These dwellings were submerged a foot or two below ground level, probably for coolness in the summer and warmth in the winter. The walls and roof were constructed of logs and brush, then chinked with mud. Outdoor brush ramadas were used for corn grinding, cooking and artistry.

The ability of the Hohokam to grow abundant crops and store huge amounts of food gave them extra time for relaxation. While other, less productive prehistoric people had to scratch out a living, these industrious aborigines designed and built athletic facilities for spectator sports. A rectangular ball park was sunk about five feet into the ground and played with a rubber ball and a grass hoop fastened on each side. Centuries later the Spanish found Indians in Mexico playing the same game. To make a score a player had to put the ball through the ring without using his hands. The game was low-scoring and much of the contest was devoted to wrestling and fisticuffs. When the game ended, the winner got possession of the losers clothes and jewelry—if he could catch him.

Plenty of leisure time also allowed the Hohokam to engage in arts and crafts. They developed a highly sophisticated multi-designed clay pottery believed by many to be the best ceramic work done in Arizona at the time. Pottery is the most durable art form from the era of the Hohokam and truly demonstrates the skill of these craftsmen-artists. The ceramics of characteristic red-on-buff color, was both decorative and functional. They included jars, bowls, pitchers, canteens, dippers and effigies and ranged in size from miniatures to huge jars that could hold more than 25 gallons. The decorations displayed delicate geometric and life form designs such as horned toads, deer, snakes, lizards, and people. Made from natural materials, the clay pottery was constructed by the paddle-and-anvil method and without the aid of a wheel. For knives, tools and other utensils, chert, obsidian and jasper were used. Stone axes were made from basalt. Monos and matates, the basic grinding tools of prehistoric peoples, were usually made from porous lava material.

The Hohokam have been called by some anthropologists, the Prehistoric Merchants of the Southwest. It is believed they acted as middlemen in a network of trade that extended from Mexico clear into the Great Lakes region.

From Mexico, they imported small bells which were hand-hewn from pure native copper and exotic birds. The latter provided colorful feathers for ceremonial events. Sea shells were imported from the Sea of Cortez. These shells were carved and ground into rings, bracelets, pendants and figures. Using pitch as a bonding agent they designed beautiful turquoise mosaics on the backs of the shells. The etching of life forms on sea shells was done with an acid juice from cactus plants. A figure or design would be drawn with pitch, then the shell was dipped into a weak acid solution. The unprotected part of the shell was dissolved by the acid, leaving the raised design or figurine. About 200 years later, this process would be "discovered" in Europe. Interestingly, evidence indicates that most of the fancy jewelry and face paint was worn by the men.

Exactly why they left remains a mystery. Did the great drought of 1276-1299 A.D. drive them out? Not likely, as their massive system of canals was substantial enough to sustain a prolonged drought. The long dry spell might have brought other, more warlike, peoples into the land of the Hohokam causing a cultural decline. Perhaps the irrigation system was too efficient, causing the soil to become waterlogged. Did the soil become saturated with salt, or did warlike newcomers drive them away? Did they leave the area completely or are their descendants the Pima and Tohono O'odham peoples of today? Perhaps there was a great epidemic decimating their numbers. Possibly the industrious, entrepreneurial segment of the culture moved on to greener pastures leaving the less-motivated behind. The standard of living of the Pima and Tohono O'odham was far below that of the Hohokam when the Spanish arrived in the 1500s. The Spanish recorded evidence of a great cultural upheaval but they, too, were mystified.

Perhaps the key to unlocking the secrets to this great culture still lies buried beneath this modern day metropolis of concrete, steel, glass and asphalt waiting to be discovered or uncovered by some futuristic civilization.

The Storied Barons
of Northern Arizona

On a cold, wet February morning in 1886, David and Billy Babbitt stepped down from a westbound A & P passenger train and took their first look at the raw, boisterous frontier town of Flagstaff. They weren't much impressed with what they saw. Actually there wasn't much left of Flagstaff, since the town had been completely destroyed by fire three weeks previous. The depot house where they stood was a converted boxcar. There was little doubt in the mind of either that the visit would be brief.

Flagstaff, at that time, boasted a population of some 600, professionally served by "able lawyers, skillful doctors, honest preachers and scientific gamblers." Lumbering, cattle and the railroad provided the main source of income for the community. It was also a favorite gathering place for nefarious scalawags along the mainline, whose only visible means of support was rowdyism. It was said that some 250 saloons were scattered along 350 miles of track. Flagstaff boasted having more saloons than all other businesses combined and they provided most of the inspiration for the rowdyism. One saloonkeeper was said to keep order in his establishment by sitting in a loft above the crowd, armed with a sawed-off shotgun.

During the building of the transcontinental railroad, an angry mob of railroad employees lynched a contractor when the payroll failed to arrive on time. On another occasion, a section hand stole a $10,000 payroll. In his haste to escape, the outlaw lost a sack containing $6,000. He was later captured but couldn't remember where he lost the money. The posse decided to hang him anyway. The unfortunate fellow made his last request, watched the noose being fitted over his neck and saw the other end of the rope tossed over the limb of a tree. While he was waiting in a melancholy mood for the jerk of the rope, a bolt of lightning struck the tree. Believing it an act of the Almighty, the posse reconsidered hanging and the man was placed in jail. Several years later, the missing sack of money was found accidentally and the man was eventually released from jail.

Hardheaded miscreants were plentiful around Flagstaff. One such character was a notorious train robber named "Doc" Smart. Doc considered himself a pretty tough hombre. But he robbed one train too many and found himself facing a life sentence at the territorial prison. Not being able to cope with confinement, Doc tried to take his own life by shooting himself in the head four times with a .38 revolver. The bullets flattened against Doc's skull and were soon extracted by a local physician who pronounced his patient "not seriously hurt."

It is no wonder that Dave and Billy were a bit skeptical on their first visit to the new town nestled near the foot of the San Francisco mountains. They had come to Flagstaff on the advice of a railroad clerk in Albuquerque. The young men from Cincinnati were looking for a place to start a cattle ranch. They brought with them the accumulated savings of the Babbitt family store in Ohio, an enterprise run by them and brothers Charles and George.

Evidently, the more they looked the more they saw potential in that part of Arizona, a region that boasted some of the best cattle country in the Southwest.

The two brothers quickly recovered from their initial shock and invested nearly all their $20,000 savings in a cow outfit east of town and thus marked the beginning of the most famous mercantile and ranching dynasty in the history of the Southwest.

The history of this remarkable family, as related to the Arizona scene, began in Ohio during the mid-1850s, when David Babbitt bought a 200-acre farm on the outskirts of Cincinnati. Here, he and his wife, Catherine, raised a family of seven children, of whom five boys would survive. These adventuresome lads, David Jr., George, William, Charles, (or C. J., grandfather of the Arizona Governor), and Edward were to form the nucleus of the Babbitt family—the "Storied Barons of Northern Arizona."

David Sr. died in 1869, shortly after the birth of Edward, leaving Catherine with the task of raising the family. As the children grew older, each assumed the responsibility of helping provide.

In the early 1880s, the four oldest brothers opened a grocery store in Cincinnati. It was here that perhaps a little fate intervened. The Babbitts had the good fortune to locate their store on a corner diagonally across the street from a

*The Babbitts of Northern Arizona: (from left) George, Charles (C. J.,
grandfather of Bruce Babbitt), Edward, William, and David, Jr.*

wealthy Dutch merchant named Gerard H. Verkamp. Verkamp
was not only a successful businessman, he was the father of
four lovely daughters. It wasn't long before romance blos-
somed between the Verkamp girls and the enterprising
young Babbitt brothers. Eventually David, C.J. and Ed all
succumbed to the charm and beauty of Verkamp's daughters. A fourth brother, George, came close to marrying a
Verkamp girl, but instead married the daughter of another
local merchant. Billy remained a bachelor until 1915, when
he married an employee in the company.

When C.J. and Billy Babbitt first arrived in Flagstaff,
neither had any real knowledge of the cow business. They
had heard stories of the vast fortunes accumulated in the
fabled West and like many others of their time, were determined to pull up stakes and go west in search of prosperity.

After a careful examination of the Flagstaff area, Dave
and Billy Babbitt bought 1,200 head of cattle from a down-
on-his luck cowman near Canyon Diablo. The rancher threw
his experienced range boss, Sam French, in on the deal, and
the Babbitt brothers were in business. They branded their
cows with the CO Bar, for Cincinnati, Ohio. In those pristine
days when grass grew "belly high" all a rancher had to do was
select rangeland with water on it, brand his cows and turn

them loose. They gathered in the spring and fall, sorted out their cows and shipped them to market on the A & P Railroad (Santa Fe).

In the years that followed, C.J. and Billy ran the cattle end of the business. They became the predominant "movers and shakers" of the cattle industry in northern Arizona. Always

innovating and expanding their enterprise, the Babbitts soon held controlling interest in most of the large ranches in the northern part of the state, including the Circle S, A1, and the famous Hashknife outfit. In the early 1900s, Babbitt cattle ranged on millions of acres across the heart of northern Arizona, from Ashfork on the west to the New Mexico line on the east. C.J. and Billy spent most of their time in the saddle, as active as any common cowboy. They dressed like hired hands and oftentimes were mistaken for range bums by their own employees.

C.J. and Billy were ideal partners. When the two engaged in negotiations on the sale of a new ranch to the Babbitt empire, C.J. would talk to management while Billy would mosey out to the bunkhouse and talk to the cowboys about the ranch. Later, C.J. and Billy would get together and exchange notes on what the other had learned.

Billy was perhaps the most colorful of the bunch. He never carried a revolver but feared no man. He was always bailing one of his hired hands out of some predicament and was respected by all, not only as a square dealer, but a good cowman as well.

The heyday of the Babbitt cattle empire was from 1907 to 1919. During those years they entered into partnerships, held an interest in, or financed most of the cow outfits in the area. During the 40 years after the founding of the CO Bar in 1886, nearly a hundred ranches came under Babbitt control.

A scene on the CO Bar range

"What they didn't own, they held mortgages on," one said. The partnerships worked to the benefit of both. Usually the Babbitts put up the money and the ranchers supplied the management. Small ranchers needed a partner with money. By and large, the Babbitts were benevolent landlords, giving their partners almost unlimited credit. At times this worked to their detriment. By giving their partners such a free hand with operations, it was not uncommon for some larceny to take place.

The Babbitts were probably the first in northern Arizona to run sheep and cattle on the same ranges. By World War I they owned more than 100,000 head of the wooly critters. Sheep were easier to keep track of than cattle, since they grazed close together in flocks. The working conditions were better, too. Sheep were taken to the milder climates of the Verde and Salt River Valleys in the winter and spent the summers in the cool high country ranges.

Old timers around northern Arizona used to say that the sheep on the ranges were continually reminding folks who their owners were. One said, "The Babbitts have so many sheep that if you listen to any herd you pass after you leave Holbrook, you will hear them saying Baa-ab-bitt, Baa-ab-bitt,"

Back in 1886, when the Babbitts first went into the cattle business, G.H. Verkamp sought to convince his sons-in-law on the wisdom of diversification. The cattle business was much too speculative. It didn't take a whole lot of convincing, for the young entrepreneurs were always looking for some new business venture. The senior Verkamp grubstaked David to the tune of $50,000 to enter into the mercantile business. Just a few months after the big fire, Flagstaff was three times larger than before. The whole region was booming, and the citizens were crying out for supplies. It was well they heeded Verkamp's prophetic advice, for the bottom fell out of the cattle market the following year.

As the Babbitts expanded their operations, C.J. and Billy took charge of the cattle business, David opened a lumber and hardware store. Edward was still in school back East and had not yet made the scene. George, who had remained in Cincinnati to liquidate the Babbitt interest, did not participate in the cattle or retail business at first, but busied himself with other interests. He invested his money wisely in real estate, small businesses and mining properties. He was the best looking of the five brothers, more outgoing and gregarious. Unlike his frugal brothers, he enjoyed spending money on himself and others. He was forever lending or giving money to friends in need. Old timers used to say that Dave, C.J. and Billy worked hard to earn the family fortune and George worked harder trying to give it away. His lifestyle was fitting to that of a happy millionaire. The others accepted George's ostentatious ways philosophically. "George is our rich brother," they conceded. He took an active interest in politics, holding many city and county offices, and was an advisor and confidant to Governor George W.P. Hunt, Arizona's "perennial governor." In 1920, just as his own political star was rising, George suffered a fatal heart attack. It was generally agreed that he would have been elected governor had death not intervened.

Dave Babbitt made a success of the mercantile operation almost overnight. He took advantage of cheaper rates, buying stock by the carload. Soon he was in the wholesale business, expanding to clothing and household goods. Ranchers and traders were coming in to exchange everything from Navajo rugs to town lots for much-needed supplies. By the end of 1889, Dave had built his enterprise into the largest in Flagstaff. It was time to bring the brothers into partnership, and the Babbitt Brothers Trading Company was founded. Two years later, they were the leading retail and wholesalers in the Southwest. In the early 1900s, the Babbitt mercantile operations spread to Ashfork, some 50 miles west of Flagstaff, and Holbrook, 90 miles to the east of the home office. When gold was discovered in Mohave County in 1916, the Babbitts opened stores in Kingman, Oatman and Yucca. A few years later, stores were built at the Grand Canyon and Williams.

If the Babbitts were guilty of anything during these years, it was over optimism. They were willing to invest capital in almost any interesting deal that came along. When the nation went into depression in 1893, the Babbitts found themselves vastly overexpanded, and creditors started hovering vulture-like around the company offices. G.H. Verkamp calmly informed these creditors that he would back his venturesome sons-in-law through the difficult period. When the creditors asked how far he would go, Verkamp replied tersely, "Up to a million dollars if necessary." They backed off, the Babbitts recouped their losses as the economic situation improved. Thus, Verkamp halted a financial panic without spending a nickel.

The Babbitts always enjoyed good employee relations. Company philosophy was to pay higher wages than others, thereby attracting a better class help. Just how loyal these employees could be is illustrated by an incident that took place on a dark depression day in 1893, when the Babbitts were desperately low on ready cash. Employee John Lind walked into the business carrying a black satchel; its contents consisted of his life savings. He handed the cash, some $4,000 to the astonished Babbitts, saying "It's yours as long as you need it. I'm willing to sink or swim with you." As it turned out, that was just enough money to keep the firm afloat.

The Babbitts, of course, were rightly proud of this kind of employee support. On the other hand, there were many occasions when partners and employees took advantage of the firm's benevolent generosity and there would be even greater economic reversals for the company in the future.

Although there have been several critical periods in their rags-to-riches history, there were only two major economic crises in the 90 years since the Babbitt brothers organized, but they were of epic proportion. The banks took over management of the company in the early 1920s. The Great Depression years, 1930-34, also took its toll on Babbitt operations. The visionary brothers, always eager to experiment and diversify, had overexpanded again. Because of their reluctance to let money sit in a bank, Babbitt cash reserves were always low. They were continually buying up ranches and other properties with spare capital. When a financial crunch came, they had no ready cash to fall back upon.

Another of their shortcomings, at least according to their creditors, was their refusal to "tighten up their cinches," so to speak, or let go of certain valuable properties during hard times. Several business ventures were sold off by tight-fisted, carpetbag management during those years. A prize ranch in California, the Laguna, was forcibly sold for $1.5 million. Less than a year later, the ranch was resold by the creditors for more than twice that amount.

It has been suggested that some of the large creditor banks were calling in their notes in an effort to crush the Babbitts and pick up the pieces for themselves. One outsider called it "legal robbery without a gun." Fortunately, not all the bankers were so greedy, but in the end the Babbitts were required to let the banks provide a manager to oversee their interests. The terms were tough. The carpetbag manager was DeWitt Knox, best known for his refusal to grant a loan to a young entrepreneur for the purpose of opening a second mercantile store. The young man's name—James Cash Penney.

An outbreak of the dreaded hoof-and-mouth disease struck their California cattle operation with devastating effect in the 1920s. The following year, "scab" decimated the northern Arizona herd. Hundreds of prize cattle were herded into trenches and shot to prevent spread of the disease. The cattle operation lost nearly a million dollars before it was over.

Through these difficult years and those to follow in the early 1930s, the persistent Babbitts prevailed. Always optimistic, they opened a new retail lumber yard in Flagstaff in 1931, during the height of the depression.

The general public was never aware of just how near collapse the Babbitt empire actually was. They always presented a calm, affluent profile. Their creditors, and for that matter, the U.S. government preferred to keep quiet about the economic state of the company. Their operations were far-flung and involved many people, not just in northern Arizona, but throughout the Southwest. If the Babbitt empire collapsed, the domino effect would be catastrophic.

One of the most profitable ventures of the Babbitts, year in and year out, has been the trading posts on the reservations. Since they opened a store at Red Lake in 1891, the trading post business has been a good hedge against hard times. Business is always brisk, the overhead low and profit margin good. There have been times when the company wished it had more trading posts and fewer cattle ranches. Today, Babbitt trading posts range in style from traditional, such as can be found at Red Lake, to Cow Springs where the decor is modern. The Babbitt sensitivity to native customs is perhaps reflected best at Tuba City where the design is in the shape of a hogan and provides for a Navajo-style single exit towards the east. A near disaster was averted at this store in 1920, when a Navajo who was dying commenced to take his final breath in the trading post. The quick-thinking manager assisted the dying man outside. The Navajo will not enter a structure in which a person has died. It would have been a taboo for any Navajo to enter the store again. Such an event did occur at another trading post in Navajoland. Today that abandoned building stands in decay, mute testimony of a people's adherence to an ancient tribal custom.

Time was beginning to take its toll on the five original Babbitt brothers. George died suddenly in 1920. David passed away in 1929, Billy a year later. Edward sold his interest in the family business in 1929. He had never spent much time in Arizona and was not as active a participant as the others. C.J. remained as the last active member of the original five brothers, although there was never a shortage of Babbitts in the prolific clan to help run the business. C.J. worked right up to the end. He died at 91 in 1956, just ten weeks after taking his retirement.

By the 1950s there were three generations of Babbitts on the company board of directors. During this time, the firm began to streamline operations by remodeling stores and supermarkets. On the ranch, new wells were drilled, holding tanks for natural rainfall were gouged out on the Babbitt ranges. Breeds were improved and fences constructed. A new era was dawning in northern Arizona, and as usual, the farsighted firm, not as large as in the early days, but more efficient, would take its natural place as the pacesetter for growth in the northern part of the state.

There were many explanations for the phenomenal Babbitt success. Their arrival in the region could not have been better timed. Northern Arizona was a sleeping economic giant when they arrived in 1886. No doubt the Verkamp grubstake played an important part. They fought back tenaciously from economic setbacks when others equally well-financed and more experienced failed and moved on. It took a great deal more than luck and financial backing to survive the vicissitudes of business on the Arizona frontier. The brothers were resourceful, patient, energetic and venturesome gamblers. It is doubtful that they ever seriously considered pulling up stakes and quitting.

Obviously, they wielded a good deal of clout in northern Arizona, yet that power was of a benevolent nature. They never tried to "run the town," although they could have easily, a trait rare in the annals of powerful families. There were no Babbitt mansions for tourists to gape and stare at today, for the families lived unpretentiously in upper middle-class homes.

During their heyday, the Babbitts ran thousands of cattle and sheep on some 100,000 square miles of range in three states; had the largest retail and wholesale mercantile business in the Southwest; owned a vast network of trading posts on Indian reservations; were proprietors of Flagstaff's first automotive garage and dealership, a dealership that is today one of the oldest Ford agencies in the nation; owned Flagstaff's only ice plant, bank, and opera house, a livery stable, beef slaughter house and packing plant, including a mortuary. The undertaking business demonstrates their affinity for entrepreneuring any legitimate enterprise. This was a prime example of defying the old maxim of avoiding entering into a business one knows nothing about. The mortuary opened in 1892 and the operating partner was a local character whose only prior job-related experience was that he was an ex-buffalo hunter. In spite of the man's dubious qualifications, the business prospered for years.

It has been said "God made northern Arizona and then he turned it over to the Babbitts to run." Some might question a statement so presumptuous, but it cannot be denied that for nearly five generations they have, in the words of one writer, "fed and clothed and equipped and transported and entertained and buried Arizonans for four generations, and they did it more efficiently and more profitably than anyone else."

The Outlaw King of Old Galeyville

The genesis of Galeyville, on the eastern side of the Chiricahua Mountains, was similar to many other short-lived boom towns in Cochise County.

In this case, it all started in 1880 when John Galey arrived from Pennsylvania to promote a silver mine. Since the prospect was only 60 miles, as the crow flies, from Tombstone's bonanza, Galey visualized himself as the next silver king of Arizona. He secured some financial backing and laid out a townsite. Before long, Galeyville boasted 11 saloons and some 30 other various and sundry enterprises.

The boom lasted only about a year. The silver played out and Galeyville became another metropolis that didn't quite metrop. The story of old Galeyville might have ended right there, had not a pack of outlaws led by Curley Bill Brocius decided to take up residence.

Curly Bill, whose real name was William Brocius Graham, was the bandit chieftain in these parts. He wore a white hat that contrasted sharply with his dark curly hair, black eyes and swarthy complexion. The boisterous, devil-may-care reprobate was considered a popular, swashbuckling figure by friend and foe alike, and nobody disputed his reputation as outlaw king of Galeyville, or the whole of Cochise County for that matter.

Curley Bill, who was given the nickname by a dark-eyed senorita from Mexico, didn't discriminate. He robbed Mexicans and Anglos with equal enthusiasm. It's been said the gregarious outlaw was some kind of frontier Robin Hood who stole only from the rich. If Curly Bill stole only from the rich, it was because there was no profit in stealing from the poor. His targets included trains, stage coaches and borderland smugglers. His favorite enterprise was cattle rustling. In those days, the U.S. Army was paying hard cash for beef on the hoof and nobody bothered to inspect the brands.

Curly Bill had a loose-knit partnership with Cochise County's unscrupulous sheriff, Johnny Behan. Behan conveniently looked the other way when Brocius pulled his capers; and when the sheriff's tax collector, Billy Breakenridge, came to Galeyville, the outlaw helped take up a collection from locals.

This unholy alliance almost got Curly Bill planted in six feet of Galeyville sod. When a tough outlaw from the Pecos River Country named Jim Wallace rode into town looking for a job, Curly Bill brought him into the gang.

Wallace claimed he rode with Billy the Kid in the Lincoln County War and had no love for lawmen. He declared they were about as welcome in his camp as a sheepman at a cattlemen's convention. When Billy Breakenridge arrived to collect taxes, Wallace took one jaundiced look at the deputy's badge, started making some threatening remarks and then drew his six-gun.

Curly Bill stepped in and ordered Wallace to holster his shootin' iron and apologize.

"No Lincoln County hoss thief can come in here and abuse Billy," he warned, "Breakenridge is our deputy and that suits us."

For a spell, it looked like the matter was settled. The three went into the nearest saloon and shared a bottle of ol' tanglefoot whiskey.

After a few drinks, however, Curly Bill got surly. Suddenly, he jerked his six-shooter and threatened to plug Wallace. Bloodshed was avoided when several of the boys separated the pair.

Wallace stomped out of the saloon, went to the stable, and got his horse. He rode back up the street, dismounted, and waited outside the saloon for Curly Bill. When Brocius stepped through the swinging doors and saw what was happening, he went for his gun. Wallace had already drawn his and had it resting on his horse's neck. A shot rang out, and Curly Bill went down with a bullet hole clean through his cheek.

Several members of Bill's gang grabbed Wallace and started to string him up; but when it looked like Curly Bill was going to survive, they let him go. Bill lost a couple of teeth, and had to spend the next few weeks with an awkward bandage tied around his head to keep the jaw in place. Otherwise he was no worse for wear.

Curly Bill figured prominently in many of the nefarious doings along the Mexican border in the early 1880s. He was personally responsible for rustling thousands of Mexican longhorns, and earned the dubious distinction of having his name mentioned in a number of warm-worded diplomatic notes exchanged between the U.S. and Mexico.

The outlaw's undoing came in the spring of 1882 when he mixed it up with the Earp brothers and Doc Holliday at Mescal Springs. Wyatt Earp claimed that, during an exchange of shots, he downed the outlaw chief with a blast from his twin-barreled scattergun. Curly Bill's cronies always insisted their leader was never at Mescal Springs, but was in Mexico with his sweetheart at the time.

There was so much controversy over the matter that a Tombstone newspaper, friendly to Curly Bill's wild bunch, offered a thousand-dollar reward to anyone who could produce the corpse of Curly Bill. The other Tombstone paper, siding with Wyatt, countered by offering a thousand dollars for the live body of Curly Bill. Neither side ever collected.

Three-Finger Jack Fingers The Bad Guys

Burt Alvord was a big, strapping, swarthy-looking character with a bald pate and an I.Q. that was said to be considerably less than his age, which was about 30. Alvord did have a few positive attributes. He was usually cheerful, had a sense of humor and was a mighty popular fellow in Cochise County during the 1890s. He'd been a deputy for county sheriff John Slaughter, who'd pronounced him absolutely fearless.

Burt was also pretty good with a six-shooter. Old timers said he demonstrated his prowess at beer bottles hung from a tree limb by a string. He'd shoot the string with his right hand, then draw with the left and break the bottle before it hit the ground.

His major interests seem to have been poker, pool, horses, guns and practical jokes.

One time he and a crony, Matt Burts, sent a telegram to

Tombstone announcing, "the bodies of Burts and Alvord will be arriving on the Bisbee stage this afternoon." Naturally, the locals thought the pair had been killed in a gunfight. Kind words were said about the boys and a large delegation gathered to meet the stage. Mourning changed to chagrin when the mischievous pair emerged from the stage grinning, "Our bodies have arrived. We never go anywhere without 'em."

Burt wasn't opposed to a little larceny either. One time he and a little Irishman, Biddy Doyle, staged a fixed wrestling match in Bisbee. They recruited a muscular miner who was willing to take a fall for a reasonable fee. The only soft piece of ground suitable for the event was the manure pile outside the Copper Queen Mine. In physical appearance, Biddy was a David facing the Goliath of the hardrock bunch. The odds rose to about 20 to 1 in favor of the miner. Burt and Biddy stood to make a handsome profit in the outcome. Things might have gone better if the pair had rehearsed the match and not made the fix so obvious. However, early in the first round, Biddy rolled on top of the miner and shoved his face down into the manure. The big guy called it quits amidst a roaring outcry from the crowd who figured they'd been had. During the confusion, Burt and Biddy somehow managed to grab the money and hightailed it for Tombstone.

Burt was as good with his fists as he was with a six-gun, something that inspired the city fathers in the new rough and tumble town of Pearce to hire him as constable. In no time, he'd pacified the two-fisted miners. When things got out of hand at the rollicking cowtown of Willcox, Burt was called in to tame the town. Again; he was up to the task.

I reckon things were getting too easy for the good natured constable and he felt a need to broaden his dimensions. That's when he decided to go into the lucrative business of robbing trains. He could use his job as a peace officer to screen these nefarious activities and no one would suspect. Besides he was too well-liked by the local citizenry to be accused of a crime. Also, it might be added, no one figured him to be smart enough to pull off a robbery and get away with it.

Alvord rounded up a few cronies to assist in these endeavors. He'd plan the crimes and establish alibis while they'd execute them. The gang included a pugnacious kid named Billy Stiles; Bill Downing, a surly ne'er-do-well; Matt

Burts, a not-too-bright cowboy; Bravo Juan Yoas and Three-Finger Jack Dunlap, a pair of saddle bums who'd do anything for money except work.

The first robbery took place at Cochise Station on the evening of September 11, 1899. The take has been estimated as high as $30,000 in gold.

Alvord's alibi was cleverly planned. He, Matt Burts, Stiles and Downing were playing poker in the back room of Schwertner's Saloon when the robbery occurred. Every few minutes, a porter would carry a round of drinks into the room and then emerge with a tray of empty glasses and announce to the local imbibers that Burt and the boys were having a serious game of poker behind those closed doors.

Meanwhile, Alvord and his pals exited a side window slipping into the darkness. Stiles and Matt headed towards Cochise Station while Alvord and Downing waited outside Willcox for their return. When the pair returned with loot in hand, they all returned to the saloon, re-entered through the side window and resumed their game.

When word of the robbery reached Willcox, someone suggested they notify Constable Burt Alvord, who was involved in a poker game at Schwertner's Saloon. Burt was noticeably shocked upon learning that the Southern Pacific had been held up. He immediately deputized his poker-partners and off they rode. Naturally, the trail was lost on the outskirts of Willcox.

Just to make sure the boys didn't start squandering their new wealth around town and arouse suspicion, Burt took the gold to a secret hiding place and buried it. He was feeling pretty good about his perfectly executed train robbery and the alibi he'd established. It sure looked like good ol' Burt had planned and executed the perfect crime.

However, Alvord didn't count on the persistence of Wells Fargo detectives and a suspicious lawman named Bert Grover. Grover suspected the constable of Willcox early on— perhaps he acted a little too innocent. Grover cajoled the porter at the saloon into confessing to his role in establishing Burt's alibi. But, before he could bring charges, his star witness got cold feet and left the territory. Having no other witnesses, investigators could only hope for a break in the case.

Meanwhile, Burt was feeling so confident about his debut as a mastermind of crime, he decided to plan another. This time he let Bravo Juan, Three-Finger Jack, Bob Brown and the Owens brothers do the dirty work.

The daring robbery took place at the train station at Fairbank on the evening of February 15, 1900. This time something went awry. The outlaws didn't figure on the legendary Jeff Milton being in the express car.

Posing as drunken cowboys, the five bandits opened fire on Milton as he stood in the open door of the car as it pulled into the station. Seriously wounded, Milton fell back inside. The experienced old gunfighter had the natural instinct to grab his trusty Wells Fargo shotgun as he dropped. The five desperados charged through the door just as Milton rose and cut loose with his ten-gauge. Bravo Juan saw it coming and turned his backside just in time. He caught a load of doubleought shot in the seat of the pants. He lit out on the run and didn't stop until he hit the Mexican border. Three-Finger Jack wasn't as lucky. He was hit full force.

The outlaws went away empty-handed, that is, if you don't count the Wells Fargo lead two of 'em were carrying.

Three-Finger Jack was mortally wounded; and a few miles from Fairbank, his compadres left him beside the trail to die. Back at Fairbank, a posse was organized. Trackers easily picked up the bloody trail leading to where Dunlap lay. Needless to say, the dying outlaw was much-chagrined at being left behind by his cronies and was only too willing to give testimony, not only for the details surrounding the Fairbank robbery, but the one at Cochise Station as well.

As a result of Three-Finger Jack's confession, Wells Fargo got the break they needed to crack the case and the citizens of Willcox had to find a new constable. Burt Alvord eventually did his time at the Yuma Territorial Prison. Incidentally, the recovery of the loot remains a mystery. Old timers around Willcox said that after Burt was released, he came back to town to say, "Howdy," to his old friends, then left for Central America where he bought a large cattle ranch. Who grub-staked him? *Quien sabe?* Although one can't help but wonder if he might have stamped a WF brand on the hides of those critters in honor of his unwilling benefactors. After all, Burt did have a grand sense of humor!

A Trio of
Colorful Characters

Some of the West's most colorful characters ended up in Arizona sooner or later. For some, it was the lure of the boomtown bonanzas. Others found it a refuge from the restrictions of more established societies in the East.

For DeForest Hall, it was the wide open spaces and the weather. He liked the high desert around Wickenburg so well that he changed his middle name to Wick.

Dick Wick Hall as he became known, (he needed a new first name to rhyme with his new middle name), opened a gas station out west of Wickenburg in a forlorn spot he named Salome. The Los Angeles to Phoenix highway wasn't much more than a cattle trail in the 1920s and Hall's dry sense of humor seemed to fit real well with the local climate. He was an instant hit with travelers.

Hall plastered homemade signs on the walls of his so-called Laughing Gas Station, and along the dusty road for several miles in both directions poking fun at the weather, bumps and ruts on the Arizona highways. One advertised "Free Hot Air;" while another proclaimed, "Arizona Roads Are Like Arizona People, Good, Bad and Worse." The best laughgetter was, "Smile, Smile, Smile, You Don't Have To Stay Here But We Do." The eye-catching signs provided a welcome relief to bone-weary travelers and inspired even the most cynical Californian to grin and bear it.

A desire to tell the outside world about the wondrous wonders of Salome inspired Hall to publish a newspaper called the *Salome Sun.*

His homespun stories were spiced with mythical characters such as the "Reptyle Kid," "Chloride Kate," and "Sheep Dip Jim." Soon the whole country knew of Salome, Arizona, where lived a dehydrated seven-year-old frog who hadn't learned to swim because it had never seen water.

Perhaps Dick Wick Hall's greatest contribution was in the area of leisure time activity. Unwittingly, he also discovered a way to keep the snowbirds, who flock to Arizona in the winter, off the streets. This was the famous Greasewood Golf Lynx. The course was 247 miles long and had a par of 16,394. Along with the usual golfing equipment, he pledged to provide canteens, pack mules, camping equipment and maps. "A winter visitor could spend the whole season here and play only one round of golf," he bragged with understandable civic pride.

Another Arizona character who delighted locals and visitors alike was John Hance. In the old days they used to say that anyone who visited the Grand Canyon and didn't meet Captain John Hance had missed half the show. For some 20 years, Cap Hance provided lying and lodging for the tourists. His brand of humor was a windy nature. The dudes never knew just how much of Cap's stories to believe, for he always led them down the paths of plausibility until they found they'd reached conclusions that were impossible—or were they?

Like the time he was riding his favorite white horse, Darby, near Red Butte along the Canyon's South Rim. (He gave all his mounts the same name—claimed it made it easier to remember what to call them.) Now old Darby could smell hostile Indians 40 miles away, and when he started tossing and snorting, Cap grew wary.

Pretty soon, he saw a bunch of warriors riding hard from the south. Cap put the spurs to Darby and they turned east only to find another painted-up war party coming from that direction.

Darby set up and turned the other way, but another band was whooping it up in the west. Cap Hance and Darby knew that their only way out was to jump the Canyon. They didn't have a minute to waste. Old Darby took a running start and gave a mighty leap. Up and over the Canyon they soared. About half way across, Cap let his eyes drift downward. Several thousand feet below, the mighty Colorado looked like a tiny reddish-brown ribbon twisting and winding between the steep canyon walls.

Old Darby got curious, too, and looked down. That brief glance caused him to lose his concentration, and they began to fall. Down they went like an elevator gone berserk. The canyon walls were sliding by in a blur as Cap and Darby gathered speed on the descent.

Cap knew the only way the pair could survive the fall was to pull up on old Darby. He'd trained that horse since he was a colt, and everyone agreed Darby was the best reined horse in Arizona—or the whole West for that matter.

Cap took a firm grip on those leather reins and hollered, "Whoa, Darby!"

Well, old Darby responded to his master's command and pulled up short—just two feet from the canyon floor.

Hance and Darby glided safely down those last two feet.

Captain Hance (nobody knows why they called him Captain-it just seemed to fit) came to the Grand Canyon in the 1880s to go prospecting. Whatever luck he had as an argonaut was far out-shadowed by his success as a story-teller and trail guide for tourists visiting the Grand Canyon in the days before the arrival of the railroad.

Captain Hance's career as a yarnspinner was launched one day when he was lecturing to a group of tourists. He'd lost part of his index finger in an accident and a lady tourist asked, "Why, Captain Hance, how did you lose the tip of your fingers?"

Cap paused and stared at the missing part of his finger as if noticing it for the first time, then replied, "Why, ma'am, I reckon I plumb wore off the end of that thing pointing out the purty scenery out here over the past 30 years."

The audience loved it, and from that day forth Cap Hance's reputation as a windjammer grew. Visitors who didn't get a chance to be victimized by his windies felt shortchanged. Next to the canyon itself, Cap was the main attraction.

Sometimes Cap Hance's whoppers almost got him in a heap of trouble. Like the time a stranger asked him how the deer hunting was around the South Rim.

"Why, shucks," Cap replied, "I went out this morning and killed three all by myself."

"That's wonderful," the stranger exclaimed. "Do you know who I am?"

"No, I don't," Hance admitted.

"Well, I'm the game warden."

Undaunted, the captain snorted, "And do you know who I am?"

"No, I don't," the game warden said

"Well," came the reply, "I'm John Hance, the biggest damn liar in these parts."

During inclement weather, a layer of dense fog sometimes fills the canyon from rim to rim. Cap used to tell of the times when he and Darby rode across the fog bank to the North Rim. On one occasion, when they were about midway, the fog began to lift. Old Darby hurriedly jumped from one patch to another trying to reach the rim, but soon ran out of fog, slipped through a hole, and landed on top of Zoroaster Temple. Cap and Darby were marooned out on that rocky monolith for four weeks before another blanket of fog covered the Canyon. "It was a light fog," he later recalled, "but by then old Darby and me were a whole lot lighter, too."

Perhaps Cap Hance's greatest saga concerned a band of hard-bitten rustlers who stole his team of prize mules. The matched set of long-eared critters was Cap's pride. There wasn't anything the mules wouldn't do for him. Naturally, he was heartsick when he went out to the corral one morning and found them missing. He saddled up old Darby and rode out to pick up the trail. The outlaws had set a path toward Ashfork, down on the Santa Fe main line about 60 miles south of the Canyon.

About sundown of the third day, Cap's keen senses picked up the smell of meat cooking over hot coals. He got off Darby and crawled over a rise for a look-see. Nestled in a thick juniper grove was an old barn. The outlaws, unaware they were being followed, had stopped to eat.

Cap's joy at catching up with the rustlers quickly turned to sorrow when he saw the hides of his prize mules nailed to the wall of the barn. Why, that pack of rascals had skinned his pets and were sitting around the fire getting ready to eat them!

There were five of the outlaws. All were well armed; and the meanest looking scalawags you ever saw. Cap not only felt it was his duty to capture that wild bunch but also figured he owed it to his poor mules to avenge their demise!

This called for some mighty fast thinking, and Cap rose to the occasion. He waited patiently for the rustlers to fill their mouths with mule meat, then, just as they were swallowing, he hollered, "Whoa, mule!"

And would you believe it? Those obedient mules heard their master's call and stopped right in their tracks.

While those outlaws were squirming on the ground trying to clear their clogged throats, Cap Hance walked into camp and disarmed the whole bunch.

Captain Hance gained his reputation as a master of the art of pulling legs attached to tender feet and Dick Wick Hall won renown for his dry Arizona humor. Both were characters inspired by tourists. Going back a few years, before the mass migration of greenhorns, Joe Felmer was one of Arizona's better-known personalities.

Felmer did a little scouting for the Army around old Camp Grant in the 1870s and had a little ranch a few miles from the post. He had been married to an Apache woman for a time and considered himself able to match wits with the wily warriors in every way.

One day a small band ran off with some of his livestock and Joe decided to get even. His fertile mind had devised a scheme that would teach the Apaches a lesson they'd long remember. The army was auctioning off some worn-out mules and Joe decided to buy the most useless one of the lot.

The mule he picked was a stubborn, sore-backed brute named, Lazarus.

Felmers friends laughed as he led Lazarus away.

"Ol' Lazarus thinks he's retired," a friend opined, "He won't move an inch with anybody on his back."

"That's jest what I'm hopin' for," Felmer replied, "The Apache that tries to ride off on him is goin' to be a sittin' target."

Felmer staked ol' Lazarus out near the house and waited. Sure enough a few days later he spotted not one, but three Apaches atop the mule. The one in front had fashioned a bridle, while the other two were digging their heels into Lazarus' hide. True to form, the mule refused to budge.

"I've got 'em now," Felmer laughed, reaching for his rifle. Just as he was about to take aim, the warrior closest to the rear strung a horsehair rope up under Lazarus' tail and started sawing back and forth. In a flash, ol' Lazarus' eyes lit up and the vigor of his younger days was miraculously revived. Felmer never got off a shot. The ol' mule was last seen galloping through the desert, jumping arroyos and dodging cactus with three Apaches hanging on for all they were worth.

Those Magnificent Men In Their Driving Machines

Back in those halcyon days, when getting someplace was an adventure, daring drivers ran road races across the Arizona desert to promote the building of better highways. It's hard to believe but as recently as 1929 Arizona had less than 300 miles of paved highways. In 1908 promoters began staging road races between Los Angeles and Phoenix. Billed as the Cactus Derby, they attracted such racing daredevils as the legendary Barney Oldfield, Olin Davis and Lewis Chevrolet. Drivers vied for a $2,500 prize and the title, Master Driver of the World.

The prize money wasn't that important—they left more than $50,000 in auto parts scattered across the desert between Los Angeles and Phoenix. It was the lofty title they sought.

Cactus Derbies were staged from 1908 to 1914 and followed a variety of routes. One passed through Barstow, Needles, Ashfork, then turned south to Prescott, Skull Valley, Wickenburg and Phoenix. Another went to Blythe, forded the Colorado River on a ferry, then on to Salome and Phoenix. An alternative route went from Palm Springs to Brawley and Yuma before heading for Phoenix, now billed as the Speed Capital of the World.

Keep in mind there weren't any garages or service stations on the 500-mile stretch of barren desert. Drivers strapped on spare parts and gas cans for the long journey. They raced against the clock so each evening the race ended in some town and the cars were impounded under guard in a local corral to keep mechanics from making repairs. The 1908 race was won by a steam-powered car (much to the chagrin of gas-powered enthusiasts) in the time of 30 hours and 36 minutes or an average speed of 17.6 mph. The most exciting race in the series was the last one held in 1914. Mack Sennet and his Keystone Kops couldn't have done it any better.

The three-day race began in Los Angeles in a driving rain. Spectators, promoters and boosters traveling by rail, on the Howdy Special, rode along to enjoy the spectacle. Each night, boosters wearing colorful costumes of red and black along with a cap with the word, Howdy, emblazoned across the front, took possession of the town, partying until the wee hours then re-boarding their train to the next overnight stop.

East of Needles, the drivers used the Santa Fe railroad bridge to cross the Colorado River. Planks had been spread across the ties and any driver who slipped off was guaranteed a rough ride, not to mention a bent rim and flat tires. Lewis Chevrolet missed the planks and nearly destroyed his auto before reaching the other side.

Near Kingman, Bill Carlson's Maxwell broke down. He walked into town for spare parts and when he returned, thieves had stripped his auto. (Some things never change).

Chevrolet, driving (you guessed it) a Chevrolet, after a harrowing ride across the Colorado that nearly took him out of the race, was done in by a overly helpful sheepherder at Seligman. Drivers used the same type cans for gasoline as they did for water. When he stopped to gas up, the friendly herder offered to help. Unwittingly, he filled the gas tank with water.

Olin Davis went out of the race when his car did a swan dive off a mountain road in Copper Basin, south of Prescott.

The redoubtable, cigar-chomping Barney Oldfield in his mud splattered white Stutz Bearcat raced into the fairgrounds at Phoenix in a cloud of dust to finish first. He almost didn't make it though, as his engine flooded crossing New River and he had to hire a team of mules to pull him out.

Bill Bramlet and his Cadillac provided the most dramatic finish. Had there been a prize for perseverance, he'd have won hands down. Bill rolled his car down a steep hill outside Prescott. Fortunately, the car landed upright. Near Wickenburg he got stuck in quicksand; and, just outside Glendale he slid into a fence and broke his steering mechanism. The resourceful driver grabbed a couple of fence posts and tied them to the front wheels. By pulling the posts in unison, he managed to steer the car down Grand Avenue to the fairgrounds for a 5th-place finish. Out of 20 entries, only seven finished the 696-mile race.

That night, a gala celebration was held in the Adams Hotel. Barney Oldfield was awarded the diamond-studded medal proclaiming him, Master Driver of the World, and optimists speculated that one day the automobile would pass from the hands of the professional drivers and the novelty of the upper classes to an essential fixture in the lives of the common folk.

Early Day Prospecting In Old Yuma County

About 20 miles up the Gila River from Yuma, the community of Dome basks in the desert sun. It's pretty quiet around here these days—a far cry from that prosperous time in the late 1850s when the boisterous boomtown of Gila City boasted some thousand rough and tumble prospectors. It was Arizona's first gold strike, and the town set the style for other mining camps over the next few years.

Journalist J. Ross Browne, who greatly influenced the style of Mark Twain, wrote of Gila City's heyday in 1859:

> "Enterprising men hurried to the spot with barrels of whiskey and billiard tables; Jews came with ready-made clothing and fancy wares, traders crowded in with wagon loads of pork and beans; and gamblers came with cards and monte tables. There was everything in Gila City within a few months but a church and a jail . . ."

Oldtimers used to say, "when the gold ran out, so did the miners." At last, the rich placer diggings began to play out, and the residents of Gila City packed up and moved on. About that time, the Gila River went on a rampage, overran its banks, and delivered the *coup de grace* on what was left of Gila City.

Browne revisited the site during a tour of Arizona in 1863, a year after the flood, and dryly noted the erstwhile boomtown consisted of "three chimneys and a coyote."

But already there had been another big strike not far away. In January, 1862, famed mountain man Pauline Weaver found rich gold placers while trapping on the Colorado River a few miles north of what would become the site of Ehrenberg. Weaver cached a few nuggets in the hollow quill of a goose feather. Shortly afterward, near Yuma, he showed his gold to Jose Redondo, who set out immediately for the new El Dorado. Redondo's first shovelful of dirt panned out a little over two ounces in gold. Thereafter, gold nuggets weighing more than 20 ounces each were apparently fairly common. Another member of the party, Juan Ferrera, was the luckiest of all, In the gulch that bears his name, Ferrera plucked a nugget weighing 472 ounces.

The Redondo party named the town that sprung up nearby, La Paz, for it was believed Weaver had made his discovery on January 12, the day honoring our Lady of Peace.

Within a few weeks, hundreds of devil-may-care miners pitched their tents and staked out claims around La Paz. "The population," wrote a California journalist in 1863, "is the worst mixture of Indians, Mexicans, Pikes, and white men from all parts of the earth, I ever saw."

Thieves, when apprehended, were dealt with severely. Isaac Goldberg, a pioneer merchant-freighter, described the punishment given on one instance:

> "Shortly after my arrival, a thief, who had been stealing from stores and other places, was caught. There was, of course, no law officer to confine and try the culprit, so the miners and citizens held a meeting and sentenced him to receive 25 lashes. These were promptly and lustily given. After the affair was over, they handed him five dollars in cash, telling him that if he dared to again visit the settlement he would receive a double dose of the same 'back medicine.' You may be sure that the rascal did not return, and that the community was no more troubled by thieves. We could leave all our property unguarded and yet not miss a single cent's worth of anything."

Petty thievery may have been curtailed in La Paz, but a hard look, argument, or the slimmest suspicion of a misdeal was apt to bring the hammer down on 40 grains of black powder. Street fights and saloon brawls were as common as cuss words at a muleskinners' convention. It's claimed that the western-most shooting scrape of the Civil War occurred at La Paz, when a Southern sympathizer shot and killed two Union volunteers.

Those lofty mountains northeast of Yuma, called the Kofas, are the best example of an acronym among Arizona place names. Kofa is derived from the King of Arizona Mine, which ran an operation there in the 1890s. The company used a branding iron to stamp its mark on company property. The brand, K of A, became Kofa, and a new name was born.

Arizona Place Names

Why'd They Call It That?

Long ago, Arizona settlers felt inspired to attach names to the special places they found. Sometimes they achieved palpable immortality by naming it after themselves; and sometimes it backfired.

Like the time Henry Mortimer Coane was running a small store in the Verde Valley. Folks wanted to use the place as a post office, so Coane filled out the paperwork and applied to Washington and requested it be named Coaneville after himself. Much to Mr. Coane's disappointment some bureaucrat got the letters mixed up and the place was officially named Cornville.

Contrary to logical assumption, Arizona towns Forepaugh, Cowlic, Hereford, Land, Light, Love and Snowflake were, in fact, named for people. Even Pinetop wasn't named for the trees, but for a tall bushy-haired fellow who ran a saloon there in the 1890s.

Fry, located in the foothills of the beautiful Huachuca Mountains in Cochise County, was named for Oliver Fry. During the 1950s, local promoters changed the name to the more mellifluous-sounding, Sierra Vista. "Who in their right mind," they reasoned, "would want to move to Fry, Arizona?"

The original name for Bowie was Teviston, for James Tevis, an early Arizona adventurer who donated the land for a town-site and a railroad right-of-way. However, a railroad official named Bean suggested the town be named for him. "Shucks," Tevis retorted, "these folks eat beans three times a day and they've had all they can stand." Mr. Bean failed to see the humor and retaliated by insisting the railroad call the place Bowie Station for nearby Fort Bowie. Later it was shortened to just plain Bowie.

The question, "Why are you living way out here?" was asked so often of folks residing in a tiny, remote desert community east of Ajo, that they felt inspired to name the place Why. And now everyone should know why—but they still ask.

Among the place names that fit into the department of Redundancy-Redundancy are: Table Mesa (*Mesa Mesa* or Table Table); Picacho Peak, (*Picacho Picacho* or Peak Peak); and Rillito Creek (*rillito* means little river). The Navajo's contribution in this category is Tsegi Canyon at Navajo National Monument. *Tsegi* is Navajo for canyon.

It's a rare case indeed when the government publicly admits a place name mistake but it happened once in Pima County. In 1910, government surveyors confused this mountain for Rincon Peak. When the error was discovered they shrugged and named it Wrong Mountain.

Women have played a prominent role in some of Arizona's place names. The town of Sedona was named for Sedona M. Schnebly, a member of an early-day family in the Verde Valley.

And Mount Lemmon, near Tucson, was named for Sara Plummer Lemmon who was the first white woman to climb to its summit. She made the trip on her honeymoon and did it again when she was 70 years old. It is the only mountain in America named for a woman who actually climbed it.

When polygamy was outlawed in Utah, several old patriarchs refused to give up their extra wives so they moved them across the line into Arizona and established a town called Fredonia. *Doña* is Spanish for Mrs. and free is self explanatory. "Free Mrs." is still a thriving community today on the Arizona-Utah border.

Uncle Jim's Last Gunfight

The old West was fading from reality into the realm of myth by the mid-1920s. Most of the bonafide gunfighters were gone and Hollywood took up the chore of telling how it really was. Tom Mix was earning over $17,000 a week performing super-human feats from atop his famous horse, Tony, and the public loved it. Nobody seemed to care much for the way it really was out in lotus land, so Americans were fed a heavy dose of tight-trousered, fast-drawing, hard-riding heroes.

As late as 1928, a few of the real straight-shooting lawmen of old still walked the beat in Arizona and one of them was Jim Roberts. Uncle Jim, as folks called him, was almost 70 and walked with a stoop. The older folks around Clarkdale remembered him as the deputy sheriff in the rough and tumble town of Jerome nearly 40 years earlier. Singlehandedly, he'd tamed the town taking on all trouble makers with fearless abandon.

One night three men holed up on the outskirts of Jerome after killing another in a card game. They sent a defiant message to Roberts and his young deputy to "come and take 'em."

"You take the one in the middle and I'll get the other two," Roberts said quietly as the two moved towards the desperados. Suddenly the young assistant's hands began to tremble. Roberts looked at him and said in a kind but firm tone, "Get out of the way, sonny, and I'll take 'em all." Moments later all three killers were down.

Before his long and illustrious career as a lawman, Jim Roberts was deeply involved in the notorious Graham-Tewksbury feud at Pleasant Valley. Roberts rode with the Tewksburys and all agreed he was the most dangerous man with a gun in either faction.

But that was a long time ago and now the legendary gunfighter of the Old West was a kindly, old gentleman known around Clarkdale affectionately as Uncle Jim.

Youngsters had heard all the stories of this old man but in their eyes he didn't seem to fit the image of a Tom Mix, or even a Buck Jones or Hoot Gibson. Why, Uncle Jim didn't even carry his nickel-plated revolver in a fast-draw holster—

he packed it in his hip pocket. When they asked him to tell stories about the Pleasant Valley War or his famous shootouts as a lawman, he'd just smile and change the subject. Another thing that bothered the kids was that Uncle Jim didn't dress like a cowboy. One day, after much prodding, he agreed to draw his famous revolver.

Those used to seeing Tom Mix fast draw and fire 40 rounds from his six-shooter without reloading were disappointed when the old man reached into his hip pocket and with slow deliberation, drew the six-shooter and gripping it with two hands, carefully aimed at an imaginary target.

Well, needless to say, there were more than a few youthful doubters in the gathering. "Maybe," they thought, "those stories about Uncle Jim were nothing but tall tales." To some it was kind of like waking up on Christmas Eve and catching Santa Claus kissing your mother next to the Christmas tree.

All those doubts about Uncle Jim were laid to rest one day in 1928 when two Oklahoma bank robbers held up the Bank of Arizona (First Interstate Bank) in downtown Clarkdale. The two walked out the door with $40,000 in payroll—the largest heist in Arizona history at the time. Old Jim Roberts was making his rounds just as the two robbers jumped in their getaway car and started to speed away. One turned and fired a shot at the old man. With that same slow deliberation, Roberts reached into his hip pocket, drew his nickel-plated revolver and with a firm two-handed grip, took a bead on the driver.

The pistol bucked in his hand as a bullet struck the driver in the head. The car went out of control, jumped the curb and landed against an electric pole. The other outlaw climbed out of the wreck, stunned. He took one look at the old man with the two-handed pistol grip and meekly surrendered.

There wasn't any doubt among the youngsters of Clarkdale after that. It wasn't the clothes that made the man. As far as they were concerned, Jim Roberts could out-shoot, out-think, and out-fight Tom Mix or any of those other Hollywood shooting stars any day of the week.

On January 8, 1934, Jim Roberts died of a heart attack while making his rounds in Clarkdale. It was fitting somehow that one of the Old West's greatest lawmen, and the last gunfighter in the Pleasant Valley War, should die with his boots on. But wait a minute—one thing I forgot to mention— Uncle Jim didn't wear boots!

Graham

Index

Note: America, Americans, Arizona and Arizonans are not included in the index because they appear so frequently in the copy.

Index (continued)

Index (continued)

Bisbee street scene in the 1890's
(courtesy Southwest Studies Program)

Index - Years

The Arizona Trilogy
by Marshall Trimble — Arizona's Official State Historian

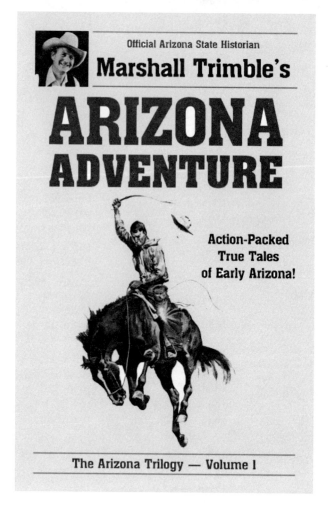

Official Arizona State Historian

Marshall Trimble's

ARIZONA ADVENTURE

Action-Packed True Tales of Early Arizona!

The Arizona Trilogy — Volume I

ARIZONA ADVENTURE
Volume 1 - The Arizona Trilogy

Daring deeds and exploits of Wyatt Earp, Buckey O'Neill, the Rough Riders, Arizona Rangers, and the notorious Tom Horn, to name a few. Read about the Power brothers shootout, Pleasant Valley wars, the Hopi revolt—action-packed true tales of early Arizona!

5 1/2 x 8 1/2 — 160 Pages . . .$9.95

The Arizona Trilogy
by Marshall Trimble — Arizona's Official State Historian

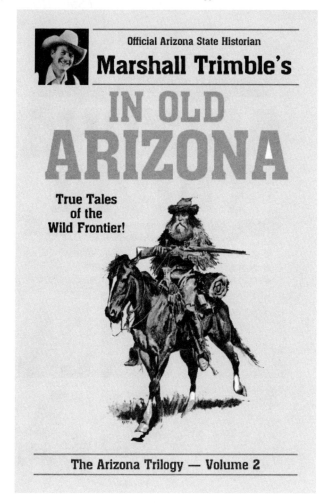

IN OLD ARIZONA
Volume 2 - The Arizona Trilogy
Southwestern tales more thrilling than fiction. History comes to life with humor, pathos and irony. Pioneer lives, bungled burglaries, shady deals, frontier lawmen, the Baron of Arizona and more!

5 1/2 x 8 1/2 — 160 Pages . . .$9.95

Also by Marshall Trimble

Marshall Trimble's Official
ARIZONA TRIVIA

A fascinating book about Arizona! Arizona's Official State Historian, storyteller and humorist challenges trivia lovers with 1,000 questions on Arizona's people, places, politics, sports, cactus, geography, history, entertainment and much more!

5 1/2 x 8 1/2 — 176 Pages . . . $8.95